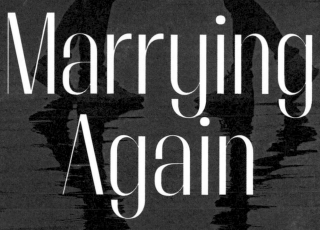

Marrying Again

52 Devotions to Prepare Your Heart and Mind for Marriage after Divorce

RON & NANCY KELLER

BroadStreet
PUBLISHING

BroadStreet Publishing® Group, LLC
Savage, Minnesota, USA
BroadStreetPublishing.com

Marrying Again: 52 Devotions to Prepare Your Heart and Mind for Marriage after Divorce
Copyright © 2023 Ron and Nancy Keller

9781424562831 (hardcover)
9781424562848 (ebook)

Stock or custom editions of BroadStreet Publishing titles may be purchased in bulk for educational, business, ministry, fundraising, or sales promotional use. For information, please email orders@broadstreetpublishing.com.

Design and typesetting by Garborg Design Works | garborgdesign.com

Printed in China

23 24 25 26 27 5 4 3 2 1

To our five wonderful, loving children:
Matt, Brigitte, Peter, Josh, and Jonathan.

To our "in-law" children:
Brandon, Sara, and Jennifer.

To our six beautiful, handsome, and amazing grandchildren:
Jacob, Julien, and Bella Rose
Kate, James, and Felix.

Contents

Introduction

Whenever a marriage ends, the people involved often feel guilt, anger, pain, disbelief, and general devastation. Then, when God brings a new relationship into their life, they feel alive and hopeful again. It's easy to assume that this "second chance" at true happiness is a gift we can simply accept with gratitude. But not so fast! Having been married does not mean that we know how to be remarried. And if one or both people are parents, having been a parent does not mean that we know how to stepparent.

If you're newly divorced, reentering the dating pool, preparing for a second marriage, or blending families, the good news is that millions of people find themselves facing these same challenges too. According to the United States Census Bureau, more than one-third of men and women have experienced divorce.[1] Most go on to remarry or enter new relationships and live together, and about thirteen hundred new stepfamilies are formed every day.[2] In fact, fewer than half of children live with two parents who are both in their first marriage.[3] These are "blended families," as they include remarried or recoupled families with children—hers, his, or shared—cohabitating.

Marrying again is tough and typically much more challenging than couples anticipate. We assure you that our personal experience was no exception. In fact, we believed we were reasonably ready and prepared for the challenges ahead. Then we attended a seminar for couples planning their second marriage, and our eyes opened even wider. We realized we had never even considered many of the predictable challenges that the leaders discussed.

We've all heard that marriage is hard work, but blending families requires even more hard work. The reality is that blended families differ from traditional families. To fail to recognize and address these differences is a common, critical oversight that results in shock, disappointment, frustration, exhaustion, and possibly second-guessing your decision to enter this new marriage.

Our experience in working as counselors with so many remarried couples and blended families over the years is that they enter these relationships with unrealistic expectations. They quickly become overwhelmed by all of the new, unexpected feelings and challenges that they simply weren't prepared for. Typically, these kinds of issues never arose in their first marriages: how to prioritize the marriage over "my" kids, how to handle conflict with former spouses, how to contend with clashing parenting styles, how to resolve financial stressors (especially if one or both parents pay child support or spousal support), how to determine what's "yours" and what's "mine," how to confront divided loyalties, how to promote unity...the list truly goes on. And couples often express feeling lost as to where to find help, resources, and support.

These statistics and anecdotes may sound daunting, scary, or even hopeless. Both of us are personally familiar with the pain, fear, loneliness, hopelessness, guilt, betrayal, despair, and overwhelming disappointment that accompany divorce. But we have also experienced and continue to live in the amazing joy that comes with remarriage. We are here to give you great hope that it can be done and that there is great joy and satisfaction in the adventure of remarriage and blending a family.

We've written *Marrying Again* to address you wherever you may find yourself today, whether you're newly divorced, dating, in a serious relationship heading toward remarriage, or already remarried. Each devotion contains a Scripture verse, a reading, a "Take Action" step to encourage reflection and personal growth, and a closing prayer. If you read this book with another person, we highly recommend that each reader uses his or her own copy.

In these pages, we share knowledge, wisdom, and skills we have learned not only from our professional backgrounds as counselors but also from real people and their real experiences, ours included. Our goals for this book are to bring you encouragement through stories and lessons, to identify the most common feelings and challenges unique to remarriage and blended families, to promote realistic expectations, and to help you connect and remain connected with yourself, with God, and with each other—one day at a time.

Please take a few minutes to write down and share with your partner three goals that you hope to reach by reading this book together. For example, your goals may be to work better as a team and to become a united front, to learn not to blame each other when problems arise, or to support each other in concrete, tangible ways. It is important to set goals as a couple, and perhaps in time, you can set goals for your family together with the kids.

You and the children you bring into this adventure are precious gifts loved by God. And this loving God will walk with you, guiding, directing, supporting, and encouraging you every step of the way. Place your trust in him, and he will unwrap the gift of this adventure alongside you more and more each day.

1

Stories

I can do everything through Christ,
who gives me strength.
PHILIPPIANS 4:13 NLT

It is a joy and a gift to marry again. It truly is a gift because neither of us planned on remarrying after our divorces. We stumbled into each other's lives as temporary coworkers. Both of us stepped back and watched as the days and months went on and as our relationship grew warmer. Eventually, we both decided that we wanted and needed to make our relationship permanent. Since 1987, I have had the privilege of calling Nancy—a faithful, generous, and creative woman—my spouse.

When I, Nancy, married in 1971, I never expected that marriage to end. Divorce was certainly never even a thought. Growing up, it was my family's moral and spiritual belief that marriage was a sacred, permanent commitment and that divorce was never an option. My parents modeled this commitment, and I remember listening to their negative remarks whenever they heard that people we knew were getting divorced.

But after fifteen years and two children, my marriage *did* end, marking the beginning of some painful years. Throughout that time, I felt judged and abandoned by my family, guilty because of my spiritual beliefs, and both stunned and numb from having to reorient myself to a life I never expected to live: that of a single parent and most likely without a life partner. But God had another plan and one that I never

11

could have imagined. His plan included a new husband, his three children, and a challenging but exciting adventure as a blended family.

With God's help, we did a few things right from the very beginning. We shared a strong relationship with God. We moved slowly, talking and listening to each other for hours. We shared agony over not being with our children all of the time, and we often held each other in tears and in prayer. We have remained partners in this great adventure called the blended family, experiencing together both great joy and pain while remaining supportive through it all. We have lived one day at a time, so as not to become overwhelmed, discouraged, or disappointed by unrealistic expectations.

It is a joy and a gift to marry again.

Now, after more than thirty-five years of marriage, we continue to enjoy the adventure. It still has its joys and pains, of course, but when we look back on our years together, we can also see all of the gifts that God brought us. We have five healthy, grown children, who enjoy good relationships with each other and with both of us, and six beautiful grandchildren.

Most importantly, we see the incredible spiritual growth that made it possible to navigate challenges with optimism and hope. It is abundantly clear that we have made it through so much together only because of God. And we still count on him and trust in his help for the years and experiences that he has for us in the future. We know he gives us his strength to do all things.

Take Action

Consider your story in brief. Is a previous marriage part of your or your partner's history? What about children? What hopes, dreams, and wishes do you hold for yourself and for your partner and children (for both the present and in the future)? What concerns, fears, or stressors do you have? Share them with your partner. What vision(s) for the future do you share?

Gracious God, you guide us on the right paths and encourage us when we do not know which way to turn. You are our strength when we are discouraged and our source of joy in good times. Help us trust in you always.

2

The Bible and Divorce

There is now no condemnation
for those who are in Christ Jesus.

ROMANS 8:1 NIV

In my many years of serving as both counselor and consultant, I, Ron, have had the privilege of working with a wide variety of people: single, married, separated, divorced, widowed, religious, nonreligious, and from one end of the spiritual spectrum to the other. Some are entirely unconcerned with the Bible's message regarding divorce, and others live in fear of it. There are countless theological arguments about divorce, all of which can be unsettling. To better understand the Bible's perspective on the matter, let's examine Scripture itself.

The Bible references the word *divorce* twenty times, and most of these references are not exactly comforting. One verse that is particularly clear about divorce and tends to be cited most is Malachi 2:16, in which the Lord says, "I hate divorce!" (NLT). It's true; the Lord *does* hate divorce. He does not wish it for any of his children. But if we, as divorced people, read this verse out of context and *only* that verse, we find ourselves in a hopeless, depressing dilemma. We need to consider it alongside Matthew 19:8, which explains that divorce became a "concession" even though it was not what God originally intended.

The teaching that tends to soften the impact of these kinds of condemning verses is that God hates sin but loves the sinner. In Romans 8, Paul writes these convincing words: "There is no condemnation for those who belong to Christ Jesus...If God is for us, who can

14

ever be against us?...Who dares accuse us whom God has chosen for his own? No one—for God himself has given us right standing with himself" (vv. 1, 31, 33 NLT). These verses in Romans should bring your heart and mind tremendous relief. They promise that nothing can separate us from the love of God expressed in Christ Jesus. Nothing!

Nothing can separate us from the love of God expressed in Christ Jesus.

This promise comes directly from God, yet so many of us look at this truth from a distance, casually writing it off as if it's simply too good to be true. We expect a hook of some kind to imply that we will surely pay for our mistakes. We might beat ourselves up over our errors and sins and feel unworthy of God's promise. But hopefully, a day will come when we accept the free grace in Jesus that God offers us. That will be a day to celebrate as one of complete closure and total freedom.

It is wise to bring closure to all matters related to our divorce so that we can live in God's promise. If you continue to experience anxiety, fear, or consternation over the Bible's message on divorce, we encourage you to consult with a counselor or pastor who can help you find closure. The National Christian Counselors Association's website[4] can provide names of counselors near you.

Take Action

Let God be God. Let him make good on all of his promises. Trust him. Let go of whatever negativity you've endured or continue to endure and seek comfort and solace in him. Draw near to him. Thank him for the grace found in Christ. Share these truths with your spouse and your children.

Thank you, Lord God, for your compassion, your forgiveness, and your grace. I know that nothing I have done or will do can separate me from your love. I am so grateful for my relationship with you.

3

God's Unconditional Love

"Never will I leave you;
never will I forsake you."

HEBREWS 13:5 NIV

Divorce can bring with it such profound loneliness. We lose our day-to-day partner and might even lose connections with friends, who are now potentially having to contend with matters of loyalty, personal beliefs about divorce, or uncertainties about what to say or do. As a result, many of us feel judged, abandoned, and alone, and we self-isolate out of sheer emotional exhaustion. This is when we turn to God and his unconditional love.

We must remember that Jesus came to bring the abundant life: "I came to give life—life in all its fullness" (John 10:10 NCV). The abundant life means that we are to receive all that God wants to give us. God forgives us for all of our failures and sins. He redeems us, he cleanses us, and his love for us is unconditional. He leads us into a new season of life, and he never abandons us.

Once we embrace the grace found in Jesus, we no longer need to justify, explain, or blame because he understands. He does not want us to suffer; he came to set us free. He accepts us as we are and loves us the same—divorce and all. Whatever others might think or say about divorce becomes irrelevant. It should no longer impact or weigh us down because there is no condemnation for those of us who are in Christ Jesus.

For both of us, divorce was considered the ultimate "bad sin" in our minds and the minds of our family, church, and others, but it was Jesus who reassured us that he would not forsake us. We clung to the knowledge that he understood our anguish. Independently, we did the necessary, important, personal work that accompanies the trauma of a divorce. Healing came, and hope was revived. The sun began to shine again. To this day, God continues to strengthen our faith in him and our bond as a couple.

What an amazing gift we have in Jesus' grace. And it is the acceptance of this gift that helps us forgive and accept ourselves and others so that we can enjoy life with hope and anticipation. This gift of grace helps us graciously receive the new gifts that God brings us each day.

Take Action

Are you ready to trust Jesus' promise that he will never leave you? If you are not quite there yet, then ask him to help you believe him. Ask him to give you the courage to move forward in life with your eyes and heart wide open.

Thank you, Lord Jesus, for the gift of your faithful and abiding presence in my life. You are my great physician and good Shepherd, and I appreciate what you have done and continue to do for me. I know that you will always be there for me and that I can count on your unconditional love.

4

Beauty from Ashes

He has sent me to bind up the brokenhearted...
to bestow on them a crown of beauty instead of ashes.
Isaiah 61:1, 3 NIV

A good friend of mine invited me, Ron, for lunch a few weeks after my divorce was finalized. Knowing this friend was a good listener and a wise man, I launched into my thoughts and feelings: "I feel like a failure. My divorce has devasted me," I confessed. "I am in great pain about my kids and not being with them all of the time. I feel like my career as a counselor has been destroyed. Like never before in my life, I feel defeated and hopeless."

I'd become the host of my own pity party, and my friend waited patiently for an opportunity to respond. "Ron, I know that your divorce is a horrible development in your life, but I also know that good will come from this. You will be a better man because of everything you've been through. You will be a better counselor and have greater credibility and compassion because you have been in the trenches with more than half of the people you see."

Here's the truth about divorce. It's a terrible, painful rupture in what once was a beautiful, love-filled, joyful union. But divorce is not the end of life. It may feel like it, but it's not. Divorce and all of the trouble that comes with it can inspire self-assessment, and that self-assessment and personal reflection can lead to positive, healthy changes in our lifestyles, attitudes, and relationships.

Divorce and all of the trouble that comes with it can inspire self-assessment, and that self-assessment and personal reflection can lead to positive, healthy changes in our lifestyles, attitudes, and relationships.

For example, a difficult but necessary question we must honestly ask ourselves is what contributions we made to the ending of the marriage. By placing our focus on our own behavior rather than on our former spouse's, we develop self-awareness, and that awareness and admission of our mistakes, flaws, and shortcomings open the door to positive change. We become able to identify parts of ourselves that need growth and change, and then we can ask God for help to do things differently in the future. This is the kind of self-assessment and reflection that lead to a rich, wholesome remarriage.

Feelings are a powerful part of the human experience, and they certainly influence our behavior, so it's critical for us to recognize, acknowledge, and process them with respect, compassion, and understanding. When we do this, we not only avoid getting trapped in the ashes of our past and our feelings, but we also become empowered to experience the beauty that God has planned for us.

One of the greatest lessons we can learn from the ending of our marriage is that we can and will survive and thrive. In fact, we can become the healthier, better versions of ourselves that God intends us to be. That's why the next five entries are dedicated to exploring some of the most common feelings experienced with divorce: disappointment, anger, guilt, loss, and grief.

Take Action

Read Isaiah 61:1–3. Now think back on your life, consider the ashes, and recognize the beauty that has emerged. Share these reflections with your partner.

Thank you, Lord Jesus, for the wisdom and encouragement that come from true friends. Thank you for pulling me out of the ashes and sharing with me all of the hope found in you. Help me see the beauty that you have created in my life and in the world. I pray that my life displays your splendor to those around me.

5

Disappointment

"I know the plans I have for you," declares the Lord,
"plans to prosper you and not to harm you,
plans to give you hope and a future."

JEREMIAH 29:11 NIV

It's often said that expectation is the root of all disappointment. While that may be true, we carry expectations nonetheless—of ourselves, our spouse or partner, children, friends, and coworkers, among others. Most of our expectations stem from our own desires and needs. We tend to assume that others not only understand and intrinsically know what those needs are and how to meet them but that they will also take whatever action is required *to* meet them. Since humans are not mind readers, you can see how unrealistic expectations set us up for disappointment.

During divorce and remarriage, we feel disappointment in many ways. It's disappointing that our first marriage did not work out. It's disappointing when friends and family do not offer support during challenging times. I, Ron, look back and realize that many of the most important people in my life simply did not know what to say or do, so they did nothing. It hurt badly at the time, but years later I have come to understand that their inaction was not personal. That greater understanding then allowed me to let go of my disappointment in them.

In my first marriage, I, Nancy, married my own expectation of marriage, or rather my parents' expectations. I never expected my marriage to be an unhappy one, so when it ended, I was deeply disappointed. The reality was that I married someone without either of us truly knowing or understanding one another or even understanding that happy marriages require a lot of hard work. We did not know how to do that work, and that, too, was disappointing. I also felt disappointed in myself for not knowing better.

God has since blessed me with a remarriage that far exceeds my immature, naive expectations. And it has been hard work—much more than I could have expected, and there have been many surprising challenges and disappointments. Together we seek God's help one day at a time, and he has faithfully guided us through the good times and the bad times: "Seek his will in all you do, and he will show you which path to take" (Proverbs 3:6 NLT). Not once have I second-guessed my decision to marry again because God gave us the confidence that he brought us together and that his doing so was a blessing.

Disappointment hurts, but we can trust the words in Jeremiah 29:11 that God understands our hurt and has good plans to prosper us and bring great hope.

Disappointment hurts, but we can trust the words in Jeremiah 29:11 that God understands our hurt and has good plans to prosper us and bring great hope.

Take Action

What expectations did you carry into your first marriage? What expectations do you have for your remarriage? Ask God to help you set expectations aside and seek his path and his will for you.

Lord, my own expectations have often led me to experience disappointment, both great and small. Help me trust your path for my life, my remarriage, and my blended family. You have good plans for me and for us, and you will not disappoint us when we put our life in your hands.

6

Anger

Don't sin by letting anger control you.
EPHESIANS 4:26 NLT

Anger is arguably the most powerful of all emotions. It can control us and prevent us from being our best. It can rob us of sleep and peace, inhibit our productivity, and make us irritable. Anger can convince us that we are right and that our anger is, therefore, justified. It can trap us in the past, attaching us to our former lives and spouses even after we think we have moved on. Anger can also be repressed or denied, which can lead to depression, tension, and even physical illness.

You may hold anger toward your former spouse, his or her family, your new partner, your ex's new partner, yourself, or your circumstances. Feeling anger is legitimate. Expressing anger in negative, inappropriate ways, such as getting even, behaving passive-aggressively or vindictively, or using cutting, sarcastic words, is never legitimate. As Ephesians 4:26 warns, "In your anger do not sin" (NIV).

In all cases, holding on to or inappropriately expressing anger has negative consequences. Holding on to anger does not change the past or create a better future. The Bible advises us not to let the sun go down while we are still angry and to "get rid of all bitterness, rage, anger, harsh words, and slander" (Ephesians 4:31 NLT). Harboring anger can also lead to isolation, as others might begin to avoid us, change their opinion of us, or simply tire of dealing with us and our anger.

If you want to move past your anger, then a good first step is to admit and share your anger with God as well as with a trusted friend or a counselor. Once you admit your anger to God, you can lean into his grace and embrace his power to help you gain control of it before letting it go.

Once you admit your anger to God, you can lean into his grace and embrace his power to help you gain control of it before letting it go.

It can also be helpful to journal about your angry feelings. Be honest and don't hold back. You might never share your writing with anyone (and that may be for the best), but getting your anger up and out of you and down on paper reduces its power. The first time that you write or share is usually the most difficult, and you might avoid doing it out of fear of the strong emotions it might evoke or other issues it might dredge up. But it gets easier each time you do it, and you loosen anger's grip on you. You free yourself from its negativity and toxicity, allowing you to focus on all the good that lies ahead.

Take Action

Make a list of things that you are angry about. Then make a list of people with whom you are angry. It's okay to include yourself on this list if you feel inclined to do so. Now go through the list one by one and ask God to help you forgive and let go so that you can leave the negative, unhealthy past behind and move forward.

Loving God, I don't want my anger to control me or my life. Help me identify and admit my anger, give it over to you, and move on.

7

Guilt

Since we have been justified through faith,
we have peace with God through our Lord Jesus Christ.
ROMANS 5:1 NIV

Guilt is heavy. As Psalm 38 describes it, "My guilt overwhelms me—it is a burden too heavy to bear" (v. 4 NLT). Among divorced and remarried people, feelings of guilt tend to be even more heightened, especially once the initial feelings of anger begin to subside. If left unchecked, guilt can haunt us and dampen every moment of joy throughout our lives.

The guilt we experience with divorce and remarriage is often directly connected to our beliefs and expectations of marriage and family or the messages we heard or read while growing up—much like our personal experiences described earlier in this book. Many of us were raised in families that actively *discouraged* divorce, so when the devastating reality of it became part of our life stories as adults, we felt immense guilt over our failed first marriage. And for those of us who began our own families, we, too, may have actively discouraged divorce in our homes, intensifying our feelings of guilt.

For some divorced people, guilt may be a natural consequence of inappropriate or regrettable behaviors in the marriage, be it infidelity, disrespect, ingratitude, abuse, or any other damaging contributor. For others, guilt is a feeling that we are simply more inclined to feel, regardless of circumstances. And then there are those of us who manage to move on and find happiness again, only to pick up a new variety of guilt to carry, believing as though we're undeserving of our newfound happiness.

However powerful our feelings of guilt may be, guilt's greatest power is that of teacher. It forces us to confront things that we cannot change, take back, or redo. It's uncomfortable to experience, but we can find solace in the promise found in Romans 5:1 that "since we have been made right in God's sight by faith, we have peace with God because of what Jesus Christ our Lord has done for us" (NLT). We now have no reason to condemn ourselves, and others have no reason to condemn us either.

Guilt's greatest power is that of teacher.

Freedom from guilt and condemnation is a gift. And in order to receive that gift, we must be honest with ourselves, admit our guilt, and ask God for forgiveness: "I confessed all my sins to you and stopped trying to hide my guilt. I said to myself, 'I will confess my rebellion to the Lord.' And you forgave me! All my guilt is gone" (Psalm 32:5 NLT).

God forgives and forgets, removing our sins "as far from us as the east is from the west" (Psalm 103:12 NLT). That's about as far as it can get.

Take Action

Ask yourself what and who triggers your guilt. Be honest with yourself when considering what actions or behaviors of yours may be causing feelings of guilt. Consider Hebrews 10:22 for extra encouragement: "Let us go right into the presence of God with sincere hearts fully trusting him. For our guilty consciences have been sprinkled with Christ's blood to make us clean" (NLT).

Loving and comforting God, the guilt that I feel may be justified, but help me to trust in your promise of forgiveness and peace. Help me hold on to your great promises about how you forgive and forget and help me bring back my joy.

8

Loss

My God will supply every need of yours.
PHILIPPIANS 4:19 ESV

With divorce and remarriage come many kinds of loss, some of which are easier to anticipate than others. For example, we expect that we'll no longer share a roof with our ex. We may also expect to move out of our neighborhood or city or, conversely, to absorb full, sole responsibility for the home that we shared with our former spouse. We may expect to face the future alone or with our kids but without a romantic partner.

Other losses are more difficult to anticipate, and you might be able to relate to the common cries we've heard over the years: "I never could have guessed how painful it would be to *not* be with my kids on a day-to-day basis...I miss hearing about their day every evening...My ex threw away sentimental items of mine without asking me, and I feel resentful about that...I was not prepared for the pain and loneliness of losing the relationship with my in-laws."

Divorce is not something that we expect, imagine, or plan for, and we often end up losing our places in our families, churches, and circle of friends. Sometimes the loss that is toughest to identify and work through is the loss of our ideal or what we thought and hoped marriage and family life could and would be. Most of us imagined ourselves growing old with the person we stood across from at the altar, believing we'd navigate life's ups and downs with them till the end.

Recognizing your loss is a natural part of the grieving process and a key component to letting go and moving on. Acknowledge what you have lost and allow yourself to feel sad about it—because it is sad. Sit with those feelings without judgment. Let them wash over you until the feelings don't feel so big anymore. Talk to God about how you're feeling and ask him for comfort.

Acknowledge what you have lost and allow yourself to feel sad about it—because it is sad.

We can always trust that God knows what we need most and will provide it at the perfect time. As Ecclesiastes reads, "There is a time for everything...a time to plant and a time to uproot, a time to kill and a time to heal, a time to tear down and a time to build, a time to weep and a time to laugh, a time to mourn and a time to dance...a time to love and a time to hate, a time for war and a time for peace" (3:1–4, 8 NIV).

Take Action

Make a list of the losses that you are aware of. Journal or share them with your new spouse, a trusted friend, or a counselor. What feelings do you associate with these losses? It can be comforting to spend time with people who can relate, encourage, and guide you through these losses, and if that appeals to you, then consider joining a local or online support group. And remember to be patient with yourself.

Loving God, you know the feelings that I have, and you are no stranger to them. Help me recognize them, make space for them, embrace them, and trust that you are walking through each and every one of them alongside me.

9

Grief

I will never forget this awful time,
as I grieve over my loss.
LAMENTATIONS 3:20 NLT

Grief comes in phases and stages, which is why it's so often called "the grieving process." The most commonly cited stages of grief include:

1. Denial
2. Anger
3. Bargaining
4. Depression
5. Acceptance[5]

Developed by psychiatrist Elisabeth Kübler-Ross to describe the stages of grieving someone's death, these same stages also describe the process of grieving divorce. Note that not everyone will necessarily experience every stage or move through them in the order that we've listed. Some people skip stages entirely or spend more time in one or two stages than they do in others, and that's perfectly normal.

Ask anyone who's experienced grief and they'll tell you that it's tough. It's heavy, tiring, and unpleasant. Still, we want to be familiar with the stages of grief so that we can maintain a sense of our place in the process. Our awareness of our grief and our progression through it can even ground us when we start to feel overwhelmed by all of the new changes, feelings, and fears swirling around and within us.

It's also fairly common for friends and family members to identify our place in the grieving process. This, too, can be helpful, as it reminds and reassures us that the things we're feeling, thinking, and experiencing are not only normal but also understandable. In turn, this reassurance and validation from trusted relationships can help us grant ourselves much-needed grace.

We strongly advise newly divorced people to allow themselves ample time to grieve the loss of their marriage fully and unashamedly before reentering the dating pool. The excitement and allure of a new relationship, although perhaps difficult to resist, might drown out your grief but only temporarily. If dismissed, ignored, or repressed, grief can creep back into your life and with the potential to wreak emotional havoc. And if you're already in a new relationship when this happens, your grief could jeopardize it by making your new partner uneasy or worried that you weren't ready to begin again. Take your time to fully grieve to avoid this common pitfall.

Even once they've fully grieved the loss of their marriages, plenty of divorced people will continue to grieve periodically long after their divorce is finalized. A friend of ours described it this way.

> My ex and I are friendly coparents, but every holiday, birthday party, or momentous occasion is impacted by the divorce and forces me to grieve it all over again. I wasn't with my daughter when she lost her first tooth, and I thought, *I would have been there for her if we weren't divorced.* But I was able to talk back to my grief and rationalize that she could have just as well lost her tooth at school and that she's still a happy, healthy kid at the end of the day.

We can feel at peace with our divorce and grieve it at the same time. It may seem tricky to hold contradictory feelings, but this kind of complexity is part of the human experience. Over time, you'll be able to move through your grief more quickly and experience it less intensely.

*We can feel at peace with our divorce
and grieve it at the same time.*

Take Action

Ask someone you trust, be it a counselor, friend, or new partner, which stage of grief they see you in. Do they recognize any of the emotions associated with the stages of grief? What stage do you feel you are currently in? Ask God to help you accept this season of life as a healthy, normal part of the healing process.

Lord, I may never forget my grief and loss, and "yet I still dare to hope when I remember this: The faithful love of the Lord never ends! His mercies never cease. Great is his faithfulness; his mercies begin afresh each morning" (Lamentations 3:21–23 NLT).

10

Letting Go

> We do not have a high priest who is unable to empathize with our weaknesses, but we have one who has been tempted in every way, just as we are—yet he did not sin.
>
> HEBREWS 4:15 NIV

It may be surprising to hear, but Jesus experienced the same feelings that we have felt as divorced people. When Jesus' friend Lazarus died, Jesus cried and experienced loss. When he saw that people had turned the house of prayer into a marketplace for selling merchandise, Jesus angrily flipped over tables. When he saw crowds of hurting people, Jesus hurt for them. He experienced disappointment, anger, guilt, loss, betrayal, and grief just like we do. This truth should help us feel less alone and encourage us to face our feelings with less fear and shame and more courage.

Once we accept that Jesus truly understands our faults and feelings, we can trust that he will not be shocked when we confess them to him. Not only will he understand and feel them with us, but he will also forgive, cleanse, and change us. With his help and his love, we can begin to set aside old feelings and behaviors and allow him to replace them with new, healthy ones.

The key, of course, is to honestly examine ourselves, identify our feelings and faults, admit them, confess them, accept Jesus' forgiveness, and trust that he truly can and will change us. That summary makes it sound simple, but it is difficult, often painful work, and no one is exempt from it. But on the other side of giving it all to Jesus and trusting him is the freedom to let go and move on.

It can also be comforting to remind ourselves that other people have experienced the same problems, struggles, temptations, and failures that we have. It feels good to share our deep human experiences with others, and it's a powerful, healthy form of interpersonal connection. I, Ron, feel privileged to have a wife and trusted friends who engage in this type of vulnerable sharing. But ultimately, I know that the greatest lifelong companion I have is Jesus. He is willing and able to sympathize with me in all my weaknesses, and this brings me great comfort.

Our willingness to put our trust in Jesus as we do this work will pave the way for a new lifestyle and new relationships, giving them a significantly better chance of being healthy. It also gives us an opportunity to learn from past mistakes and avoid some of the pain and suffering experienced in previous relationships.

Our willingness to put our trust in Jesus will pave the way for a new lifestyle and new relationships.

Now that we've discussed five of the most common feelings experienced with divorce, we hope you feel more aware of your emotions and more confident and equipped in experiencing and addressing them. Remember that all of our feelings, not just those we experience in the wake of divorce, demand respect and attention. If neglected, they're likely to stockpile until triggered, which often leads to new conflict.

In the next two entries, we'll move on to discuss the twelve stages of healing that can lead to closure and what to reasonably expect from each stage.

Take Action

Spend some quiet time alone with God, asking him to give you the courage to identify whatever you are holding on to regarding your previous marriage or relationship—faults, feelings, thoughts, and regrets. Write them down as he brings them to the surface for you. Remember that Jesus will understand, not judge.

If you feel comfortable, share what you've written with a trusted friend or person who will listen compassionately and without judgment or seek professional help. Ask God to help you forgive yourself, let go, and move toward true freedom and emotional wellness.

Jesus, give me the courage to look honestly at myself and my contributions to the breakdown of my previous relationship. Help me bring these before you and another trusting person, believing that you will understand me, forgive me, and change me.

The Stages of Healing Part 1

Anyone who belongs to Christ has become a new person.
The old life is gone; a new life has begun!
2 CORINTHIANS 5:17 NLT

Now that we understand the importance of experiencing and working through the feelings and regrets from our first marriage and putting them behind us, we can discuss twelve stages common to the healing process. Note that we have identified these stages from our professional experience, and much like the grieving process, the healing process is nonlinear, and everyone experiences it differently. The healing we seek will come gradually and in stages—some of which are predictable—and all of them normal.

**The healing process is nonlinear,
and everyone experiences it differently.**

Stage 1: Confusion. In this stage, we struggle to contend with our new reality. Feelings of disappointment and shock often prevail, and we're completely preoccupied with all the change and uncertainty. Some might experience denial. We wonder, *How did I get here? What happened to my life? What will my new life look like?*

Stage 2: Self-pity. We feel like a victim. We blame our former spouse and feel angry, traumatized, and in pain that's at times overwhelming. Our focus tends to be on ourselves and on our kids. Feelings of guilt are common in this stage as well. Unfortunately, guilt can and often will nurture and reinforce feelings of self-pity.

Stage 3: Emerging truth. We gradually begin to understand the divorce more objectively and allow the truth of our circumstances to influence and inform our perspective. We begin to sort out what happened and may feel caught off guard by feelings of sorrow, loss, and grief. Many people experience this stage the longest.

Stage 4: Abandoning denial. We give permission for the truth to emerge by no longer denying what happened or the contributions we made to the dissolution of the marriage. We begin to admit our own powerlessness and might feel ready to talk more openly with others about our pain and experience.

Stage 5: Sharing openly. We are aware of our feelings of anger, frustration, hurt, resentment, disappointment, grief, fear, guilt, and loss and are more willing to talk about them in a healthy, productive way. We may also feel more comfortable asking others for help.

Stage 6: Breaking free. We are moving closer to breaking free from our former spouse and his or her power and control over us and our emotional experience. We can acknowledge more openly our contributions to the breakdown of the marriage. We begin to move on independently.

If you find yourself stuck in or struggling with a stage (or several of them), ask God to guide you toward another person, group, or counselor who can support you in your healing journey. Remember that Christ walks with you through these stages and helps you begin a new life in him. Look forward to the freedom and joy that you will eventually experience. God is using your circumstances to shape you into a new person—the person he has envisioned for you to become.

Take Action

Read through these first six stages again before journaling about them. Which stages sound or feel familiar? Which stages have you already experienced? Which ones might you be avoiding? Which of these stages are you experiencing right now? Talk through these questions with a trusted loved one. Try to provide real examples to help you and your trusted person better understand where you are in the healing process.

Jesus, I want you to be the center of my life. I know that you love me and that I belong to you. I trust that you will walk with me through these difficult stages and help me find true healing, peaceful closure, and new life. I thank you so much for this promise.

12

The Stages of Healing Part 2

He who began a good work in you
will carry it on to completion
until the day of Christ Jesus.
PHILIPPIANS 1:6 NIV

Stages one through six of the healing and closure process tend to be unsettling, difficult, and even painful. Though not enjoyable, those stages teach and compel us to grow in a number of ways that prepare us for stages seven through twelve. And thankfully, the later stages of the healing process promise a light at the end of the tunnel.

**The later stages of the healing process promise
a light at the end of the tunnel.**

Stage 7: Acceptance. We accept the facts of the divorce rather than revisiting them over and over. We understand it as a living death—the death of a way of life, the death of our ideals, and the death of a significant chapter in our lives that we won't relive. We express our feelings without succumbing to them, and our lifestyle begins to reflect our emerging independence.

Stage 8: Awareness of consequences. We accept the consequences of our divorce and anticipate their greater impact on our post-divorce lives. We distinguish between forgiving and being forgiven but recognize that some consequences will accompany us into our new lives and may very well never change.

Stage 9: Hope. We have a new appreciation for life and feel hopeful for what it may bring. We let go of past misunderstandings, feelings, and experiences and move toward forgiveness, understanding, compassion, and closure. We ask God for grace to move on and discover his plan for the rest of our lives.

Stage 10: Serenity. We finally feel at peace with ourselves, others, and God. Our circumstances no longer control or have power over us. We are learning to live in the moment, enjoy the present, and embrace everything that it brings.

Stage 11: Confidence. We feel good about ourselves. We are confidently grounded and anticipate the future without fear, dread, or anxiety. We are, as Paul says, "confident of this, that he who began a good work in you will carry it on to completion until the day of Christ Jesus" (Philippians 1:6 NIV).

Stage 12: Ready for a new relationship. Our hearts and minds are healthy and ready for a new relationship whether we seek one or not and regardless of whether that is God's plan for us. We have closure over our previous relationship and feel secure in our relationship with Christ, who has done a good work in us.

Take Action

Assess which of the twelve stages of healing you are in right now and why. Then ask a trusted loved one which stage he or she sees you in. If the two of you disagree, then have an honest discussion about it. It's normal to feel impatient and to want to see yourself further along in the healing process than you might actually be. Ask God to help you have an open heart and mind.

If you and your trusted loved one agree that you have come a long way and are at or near the final stage of this process, rejoice and thank God for guiding you through what may have been a difficult journey. God has been preparing you for the good plan he has for you and your future (see Jeremiah 29:11). Such good news, don't you think?

Jesus, I finally see the good work that you have been doing in my life to help me put the difficult things of my past behind me. Thank you for the hope you provide and for helping me surrender to you more each day. I trust you to bring the healing, peace, and serenity that I cannot achieve on my own.

13

Relationship Readiness

"I am about to do something new.
See, I have already begun! Do you not see it?"

ISAIAH 43:19 NLT

Once we've successfully moved through the stages of healing and closure, we likely feel more comfortable looking toward the future and might even hope for a new relationship. We have good news and bad news on this. The good news is that the majority of people who divorce go on to remarry or recouple. The bad news is that the percentage of second marriages that end in divorce is even higher than that of first marriages.[6]

Why is this? There's more than one explanation, to be sure, but perhaps the most common reason is a failure to complete the healing and closure process before seeking and entering a new relationship. When we neglect to do the critical personal work, we end up carrying the same unresolved feelings, attitudes, and behaviors into the new relationship. And it doesn't take long for those unresolved issues to plague a new relationship.

When I, Nancy, look back at my first marriage, I can quite easily identify things that I wish I had done differently but was unaware of at the time. I demanded a lot of attention, and I could be self-centered and not as affirming as I should have been. These same behaviors affected my current marriage, and it was only through ongoing personal work that I learned to bring about positive change not only for myself but also for our marriage.

Ultimately, God is in charge of our relationship readiness. He has a plan for our lives, and his timing is perfect. When we surrender to God's plan and timing, we give our new relationship its very best opportunity to develop, mature, and succeed as he intends, whereas people who rush these elements often find themselves in yet another broken relationship.

A new relationship is a gift, a second chance. Move slowly and enjoy your time together. Enjoy the moments you have away from each other too. Keep the relationship and its boundaries healthy. Protect it from becoming a dependent or codependent relationship, which is an easy trap to fall into if you still feel vulnerable or hurt from your divorce.

When thoughts of marriage begin to enter your mind, think carefully. The decision to marry again must be based on more than feelings but also on information that you have gathered about each other over time: your backgrounds, beliefs, values, goals, political views, communication styles, and so much more.

How will you make decisions as a couple? How will you handle finances? What is your partner like in times of stress and hardship? What are *you* like in times of stress and hardship? If your partner has children, what is their parenting style, and how often are their children physically with them? Solid, responsible marriage preparation with a counselor or with your church is essential and will guide you in asking the right questions and developing critical understandings of yourself and each other.

Solid, responsible marriage preparation with a counselor or with your church is essential.

You need realistic, objective, third-party input so that you can make your decision to marry again with a trustworthy perspective and then build from a solid foundation. Ask family and friends what they

43

see and how they feel about your new relationship. Listen to them and, most importantly, listen to God in times of prayer.

Take Action

If you are in a new relationship following a divorce, be courageous and ask those you love and trust what they see and how they feel about it. When those who care for you see that your new relationship is supporting you in becoming the best that you can be and bringing good things to your life, then you can move forward with confidence that this relationship is a gift from God.

God of hope, I am reminded again that you have a good plan for my life. Help me to patiently set aside my own plans and, with anticipation and trust, allow you to prepare me for the life you have planned.

14

Introducing a New Partner

"Where you go, I will go; where you lodge, I will lodge;
your people shall be my people, and your God my God."
RUTH 1:16 NRSVUE

When we meet someone new and fall in love, it's natural to want to introduce that person to our loved ones, including our children. We want to share our excitement and joy, and we want to make sure that everyone gets along. But just because you feel ready to move on doesn't mean that your kids feel ready too. Let's review helpful advice on this subject.

First and foremost, take your time. Kids continue to grieve the divorce long after it happens and need time to process and accept that your relationship with their other parent is over. Many kids hold on to the hope that their parents will get back together, so introducing a new partner too soon can be confusing and upsetting. And if you've been single for a while, they might not feel ready to share your time and attention with a new person.

Children, especially young children, sometimes invest in a parent's new relationship quite readily, particularly when the new partner showers them with attention while trying to get to know them and earn their acceptance. But when children are repeatedly introduced to new partners and those relationships end, which may very well happen more than once or twice, children may eventually stop investing in new partners altogether for fear of yet another loss. This instability can negatively impact their mental health and their ability to build solid relationships of their own later in life.

Even if you and your new partner share important values, beliefs, and visions for the future, breakups are common, and kids can get caught in the crossfire. Dr. Ann Gold Buscho, author of *The Parent's Guide to Birdnesting: A Child-Centered Solution to Coparenting During Separation and Divorce*, says, "I often suggest waiting until the new relationship has been a committed relationship of at least 9–12 months duration, after the divorce is over. Many parents resist this recommendation. I explain that this gives everyone time to adjust to a new parenting schedule and the children have the time to grieve the loss of the family as they knew it."[7] Unless a relationship becomes serious enough and potentially permanent, it's best not to introduce your new partner to your children.

Unless a relationship becomes serious enough and potentially permanent, it's best not to introduce your new partner to your children.

Once your new relationship is strong, stable, and has lasted a significant amount of time, tell your kids that you have made a new friend whom you care about and that you would like to introduce them. If your children are older and can read between the lines, it's better to be forthright in telling them that you've been dating this person. Let them ask questions and answer honestly and appropriately. If they tell you they're not ready or you can see that they're uncomfortable, respect and prioritize their feelings by waiting longer.

When your kids are ready, keep the first meeting short, simple, and low key. Meet in a neutral location, such as a playground or restaurant and go (very) easy on physical contact with your new partner in front of the kids. If the meeting goes well, begin incorporating the new partner into events and activities gradually and occasionally. Kids should not feel in competition for your time and attention with a new partner.

If everyone seems to get along and enjoy time together and your new partner has children, then you might tell your children that your friend has kids too. Ask them if they would like to meet them sometime and go from there. Too much too soon will not work to your advantage.

It's highly probable that your children will eventually mention your new friend to their other parent. And chances are that you would like to know when your ex is going to introduce a new partner, so consider giving them that same courtesy in advance. Not only does this show your former spouse respect and consideration, which can improve the coparenting relationship, but it also keeps the other parent from feeling caught off guard. If your coparenting relationship is a healthy one, their other parent may even be supportive, which can help the kids feel more comfortable and open to an introduction.

Of course, consulting with your ex about this introduction is not always realistic, particularly if the divorce was contentious or your spouse still carries bitterness or harbors resentment. But remember that you have a right to move on with your life, and you don't need your ex's permission to do so.

What matters most is that you introduce a serious new partner to your children gradually, respectfully, and with your children's feelings in mind, not just your own. It is a delicate process, so ask God to guide you about timing, words, and actions. If a new, committed relationship is God's will for you, then God will help all of you come to accept one another, like one another, and perhaps build a future together.

Take Action

Ask God to guide you with wisdom, patience, and love as you bring your new partner and your children together.

Thank you for the joy and the hope of this new relationship, Lord. Direct my words and my timing and help me be sensitive to my children's needs.

15

Coping with Change

Jesus Christ is the same
yesterday and today and forever.
HEBREWS 13:8 NIV

Dating and marrying again bring change—and lots of it. Sometimes the change is big, and other times it's small. Sometimes it's sudden. Sometimes it's gradual. It can feel constant and steady, or it can feel like change comes barreling into our lives the moment that we start to get comfortable.

For people with certain temperaments, change is easy, welcome, and refreshing. These are the people always looking for a new adventure, a new perspective, a new challenge, or a change of scenery or circumstances.

People with a different temperament might dread and resist change. A big move to a new city or a different house, a change in health, or even a simple change in date night plans can trigger so many big emotions: frustration, anxiety, insecurity, fear, and confusion. These temperaments may lack the physical or emotional energy and flexibility that change demands. If you find yourself experiencing difficult feelings related to change, then you're far from alone.

The hard truth about change is that most of it is out of our control. That's why we must focus on the one who *never* changes. God anchors our soul. And with his help, we can embrace change as part of our norm. By putting our faith in him to guide us through it, we develop a positive, healthy attitude toward change, and we cultivate resilience. We develop confidence that no matter what life throws our way at any given time, we are equipped to face and overcome it.

The hard truth about change is that most of it is out of our control. That's why we must focus on the one who *never* changes.

Remember to also take care of yourself in times of transition. Do your best to remain patient, compassionate, and flexible with yourself and your loved ones. Take one day at a time and give yourself grace if the laundry piles up or that oil change light stays on longer than you'd normally let it or you find yourself ordering takeout more than usual. Talk to God. Prayer is one of our best tools when it comes to seasons of change. It provides a direct line of communication to our Creator. Talking and sharing our concerns and fears with him will bring comfort and relief.

If you have a new partner, a new spouse, or children experiencing the change alongside you, then share your feelings with them using age-appropriate language. Whether it's loss, grief, anxiety, hope, or excitement, remind them of your confidence in Christ. This models to them that you are prepared, willing, and able to identify and cope with these feelings. Your honesty may help them identify their own uncomfortable feelings about the change and reduce or alleviate any pressure they might be experiencing too. Give them a platform and space to share what's on their hearts and minds and be sure to listen carefully and attentively when they speak.

Take Action

Talk with your partner, spouse, or friend about a change that is impacting you right now. Consider including your child or children or stepchildren in the conversation if appropriate. Share your feelings and pray about it together.

Thank you, Lord Jesus, for anchoring my soul. Thank you for always being there for me in good times and bad. Please help me to trust you even when it feels like everything is changing too fast and spiraling out of control. Thank you for being my constant, reliable, unchanging companion.

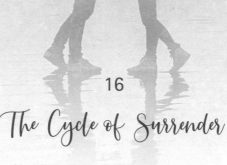

16

The Cycle of Surrender

You died to this life, and your real life
is hidden with Christ in God.

COLOSSIANS 3:3 NLT

As we grow into our new lives, it's the perfect time and opportunity to adopt all kinds of healthy new habits, particularly the art of surrender. To surrender means to abandon our efforts to control or manage our circumstances. To release ourselves from the pressure and responsibility of making things happen that only God can make happen. We experience the art of surrender in a cycle of five components:

1. Self-awareness
2. Admission
3. Struggle
4. Surrender
5. Serenity

Self-awareness takes on new meaning when we enter new relationships and attempt to blend families. Take Bob for example. For years, Bob's brothers, kids, and former wife told him that he was too controlling. They supplied examples of his controlling behavior and explained how it negatively affected them, but Bob did not comprehend or register the severity of it until he was fired from his job for the very same reason.

Self-awareness is understanding how we're wired, what emotionally triggers us, and how our behavior affects those around us. We can cultivate our self-awareness by praying, meditating on Scripture, and remaining attentive to what our friends, partner, family, and intuition tell us.

The second component of the surrender cycle is admission. Admission means verbally acknowledging our wrongdoings and failures and refusing to participate in denial, partial truths, and dishonesty about them. We make admissions to ourselves and God and often to other people. We, for example, realized we had been too critical of one of our sons, and by admitting our mistake to him, we were able to strengthen our bond with him and foster a deeper mutual respect.

After making an admission, it's common to want to neutralize or take it back by telling ourselves things like, *I can do it myself...It's not that big of a deal...This problem will go away on its own.* This is the third component of the surrender cycle, which we call the struggle. And the struggle is the result of our confronting and wrestling with our rationalizations. Try to focus on Jesus during this time.

After the struggle comes surrender, and surrender is letting go and letting God. John, a client, was trying (and failing) to force his stepfamily into a *Brady Bunch* dynamic but alienating his two children and three stepchildren in the process. John's wife pleaded with him to be more realistic, and he eventually became aware of his behavior and admitted to it. He struggled for many months before he was able to thoroughly surrender control to Jesus. If and when you find yourself in a similar situation, pray for the grace to surrender completely to Jesus Christ.

The byproduct of awareness, admission, struggle, and surrender to Jesus Christ is serenity. It is the gift of lasting peace, hope, and confidence to deal with the other elements of life. Jesus said, "In me you may have peace. In this world you will have trouble. But take heart! I have overcome the world" (John 16:33 NIV).

Notice how Jesus is honest in acknowledging that we will experience trouble (and remarriage and stepparenting is, indeed, troublesome at times), but we can take heart because Jesus overcame the world. In him we have peace. Think of it like a hurricane. On the outside, it swirls and destroys. But inside, in the eye of the hurricane, it's still, quiet, calm, and peaceful. Our external circumstances may be chaotic and stressful, but Jesus grants us a profound, unchanging internal peace.

Our external circumstances may be chaotic and stressful, but Jesus grants us a profound, unchanging internal peace.

Once you've moved through the surrender cycle a few times, you'll learn to move through it and reach serenity more quickly. After years of practice, we're able to move through it in a matter of seconds. Take it one day or even one moment at a time.

Take Action

Memorize the simple surrender cycle: awareness, admission, struggle, surrender, serenity. Practice it daily with issues big and small.

Jesus, you surrendered when you said, "Father, your will be done." Please give me the grace to surrender to your will one day at a time.

17

Common Misconceptions

He did not retaliate when he was insulted,
nor threaten revenge when he suffered.
He left his case in the hands of God, who always judges fairly.
1 PETER 2:23 NLT

Before we get into the complexities of blended family dynamics, such as living arrangements, loyalty, conflict, and discipline, let's first address common misconceptions people often have about remarriage and stepparenting.

Misconceptions make for unreasonable expectations, many of which will go unmet, and they can easily catch us off guard. We might blame ourselves or feel insulted, become confused, frustrated, or discouraged when the reality of our new relationship doesn't live up to our expectations. It's better to know what's more likely to occur and what's wishful thinking so that we can better prepare and adjust our expectations. The following are just a few of the many unrealistic expectations or misconceptions that remarried couples and stepparents tend to have.

Once our adult children have moved out of the house, they are on their own and will not be a factor in our remarriage.
Adult children are just as much, if not more, of a factor in a stepfamily than children living at home. Our parenting takes on a new dimension once our children grow up and move away. In some cases, our children

need us more than ever, so be prepared and available. Read our entry "Adult Children" for more on this.

Every negative experience, poor choice, or challenge that my child faces is a consequence of my divorce and remarriage.
Children will experience tough things regardless of their family structure, be it a nuclear family or a blended one. Divorce can certainly be one of those tough things but avoid placing too much emphasis on it or wallowing in unproductive guilt. Children are resilient when they have loving, supportive parents.

I'm already a parent, so I know how to stepparent.
Stepparenting is never easy, and our experience as parents does not necessarily translate. Yes, we want to befriend our stepchildren, but we need to understand that it will take time, perhaps a long time, for them to trust us. We also need to earn their respect before we can attempt to parent them, especially if the child already has two parents.

Because we love each other, I'm confident that my partner and his kids will accept and love my kids and me too. We'll soon become one happy, blended family.
This might become a reality for some blended families, but for most families, it will take a substantial amount of time and requires hard work and insight. Many family advocates agree that it takes an average of five to seven years to fully blend a family.[8] That is much longer than most people expect, so be patient.

It takes an average of five to seven years to fully blend a family.

Because I am an adult, I can and should expect respect from my stepchildren.
Children often do not even understand the concept of a stepparent, so we must earn their respect. We earn it through our behavior and

relationship-building. It may take a long time before we feel respected by stepchildren, especially if the children have been wounded by a person in authority. Until we establish a relationship with them, we cannot expect their respect. We'll touch more on this in the upcoming chapters on loyalty and discipline.

My partner and I should always agree on how to make decisions, including how we raise our children.
Because you and your partner were raised in different homes with different values and expectations, you will certainly have different perspectives on how to make decisions, especially related to how you will raise your children. Remember that every child is different and has unique needs and therefore needs to be parented accordingly. Accept this fact and then decide together how you will address and respect differences.

My new stepkids will come to love me and appreciate having me in their lives.
The reality is that your stepchildren may never show you love and appreciation. Continue to do the right things and love them anyway but, again, without expectation.

Take Action

Discuss your parenting beliefs with your partner. Then discuss your stepparenting expectations for yourself and your partner and identify where the two of you agree and disagree. What can the two of you do to remain a united front moving forward?

Lord, give me the courage to accept the realities ahead of me rather than my idealizations. Help me have the patience to take the high road and do the right thing no matter how wrong or unfair it may seem, trusting that you've got this and always judge fairly.

18

Predictable Issues

Dear brothers and sisters, when troubles of any kind come your way, consider it an opportunity for great joy. For you know that when your faith is tested, your endurance has a chance to grow. So let it grow, for when your endurance is fully developed, you will be perfect and complete, needing nothing. If you need wisdom, ask our generous God, and he will give it to you. He will not rebuke you for asking.

JAMES 1:2–5 NLT

Throughout our many years of leading and participating in couples counseling groups, we've become familiar with the primary marital issues that remarried couples face. We'll discuss each of them at length in later chapters, but we've summarized them below as a preview. Keep in mind that this list is not to overwhelm or discourage you but to attempt to normalize the challenges ahead of you.

- Differences in temperament
- Differences in needs, both emotional and sexual
- Differences in communication styles
- Competing loyalties
- Differences in parenting styles, particularly when it comes to discipline
- Financial matters
- Legal matters, such as prenups, wills, and child custody

Most people tend to avoid confronting these issues to avoid conflict, hoping that, in time, they'll resolve themselves. But we can't live in denial. Unresolved issues haunt us, so avoiding necessary conversations only delays resolutions, preventing us from enjoying the freedom that comes with living openly and honestly with one another.

Avoiding necessary conversations only delays resolutions.

Instead of denying our fears and our emotions, like so many of us were taught to do, we need to trust and follow our intuition when it alerts us that something doesn't feel quite right. From there, we need to share our concern with our partner so that it can be addressed. As uncomfortable as it may be to share our feelings and fears, this kind of vulnerability will take us a long way when anticipating and talking through these predictable issues together.

If we want to have a loving, respectful, successful remarriage, we must learn how to put our cards on the table and work through challenges together. Skip ahead to chapter 21, "Practicing Communication," if this feels daunting. As our Scripture verse for this chapter promises, our troubles are opportunities for growth.

Take Action

From the list of issues at the beginning of this chapter, select the two that are most difficult for you right now. If none of those issues presently concern you, select any two that come to mind. Share with your spouse how you're feeling about those issues and what makes them difficult for you. Together, come up with one action that you can take to ease the stress associated with each issue. Make a commitment to pray for each other's concerns. Revisit the subject again in a week to evaluate your progress and come up with new actions if need be.

Lord Jesus Christ, we are aware that we have issues that we need to manage. Thank you for making us aware of them. Give us the courage, strength, and patience to work through them with your help so that we can have a rich, peaceful, fulfilling marriage and family life.

19

Identifying Temperaments

You created my inmost being; you knit me together in my mother's
womb. I praise you because I am fearfully and wonderfully made...
All the days ordained for me were written in your book before one of
them came to be.

PSALM 139:13–14, 16 NIV

Nancy and I leased sailboats for years, and one of the first things we
had to do when boarding a leased boat was to conduct a thorough
inventory: What equipment did the boat have? What condition was it
in? How easy or difficult would the boat be to sail? How fast could it
go? What combination of sails would be best? This inventory, while tiring at times, was essential to a successful and fulfilling sailing retreat.
Similarly, a solid understanding of yourself and your spouse is essential
to a successful and fulfilling marriage.

Performing an inventory of yourself and each other is useful for
many reasons. It gives you a greater awareness of your strengths and
weaknesses. It reveals what your negotiable and nonnegotiable needs
are. It tells you what sets you off, what brings you joy, and what environments you thrive best in. This personal data will also help you build
a strong bond with your partner and one that is based on fact, not
conjecture. Such information is critical and much needed in remarriage and blended family dynamics because of all the extra moving
parts that come with these relationships.

We can only love what we know, so the more aware we are
of ourselves, the better we know ourselves and the better we know

each other, and the healthier we are. We can only understand, accept, appreciate, and respect others to the degree that we have done that for ourselves, which is why self-acceptance is essential.

One of the ways we help our clients to know and love themselves and their partners better is to help them understand not only their own temperament but also their partner's. The concept of temperament has been with us for thousands of years, so it's no surprise that most philosophers, theologians, counselors, and ministry leaders agree that we all have an inborn "design" of qualities, perspectives, modes of operation, biases, and ways of being that we call temperament. And that unique and specific temperament was given to us by God.

Our temperament is our innermost self, our soul, and it never changes. It is the consistent part of us that gives us stability and freedom to be who we truly are, and it comes with its own strengths, weaknesses, and nonnegotiable needs. When the needs of our temperament are met, our life is rich, and we thrive.

When our temperamental needs are unmet, we flounder, become anxious, irritable, upset, frustrated, and difficult to live with. We must know our own needs and take the appropriate steps to make those needs known so that they can be met, and we must know the needs of our spouse and our role in appropriately fulfilling their needs too.

It's also important to note that temperament differs from personality. Our personality is how we express ourselves to others and behave around them, which may very well change as our circumstances, environments, and relationships change. That is, many of our behaviors are learned but do not necessarily represent our true temperament.

Great joy can be found in truly knowing ourselves and each other. And by understanding each other's temperaments, couples are equipped to build strong communication skills, eliminate conflict before it begins or trace its origins when it inevitably happens, and effectively resolve it. And the deeper our relationship with Jesus, the more we will appreciate who we are and who our spouse is because of how God created us and what he has done and continues to do for us.

By understanding each other's temperaments, couples are equipped to build strong communication skills, eliminate conflict before it begins or trace its origins when it inevitably happens, and effectively resolve it.

Take Action

Repeat this to yourself today: I understand, accept, appreciate, and respect myself and my spouse. Thank God for creating you with a unique temperament and unique strengths and weaknesses.

Lord, help me to not only recognize and use my strengths to your glory but also to turn to you in times of weakness. Help me know my needs and those of my spouse and to meet those needs with your help.

20

Meeting Needs

"A new command I give you: Love one another.
As I have loved you, so you must love one another."
JOHN 13:34 NIV

Now that we understand the concept of temperament, let's discuss how to work with it. For many years, we've had our clients complete the Arno Profile System. It's a faith-based counseling tool and process that provides a remarkably accurate personal profile containing essential, specific information on a person's God-given characteristics.[9] We've found that it helps us better counsel and encourage our clients by providing helpful input for remarriage and blended families. Put simply, it takes a lot of the guess work out of how to best love one another by identifying a person's needs.

The remarriages that are the most successful are the ones that know how to navigate difficult times while still being able to express their needs and have them met. Many, maybe even most, of the couples we have counseled do not know their own needs let alone their spouse's. Some, on the other hand, know their needs but do not know how to express them, which means their spouse is unlikely to know how to meet them. Others dismiss their needs as irrelevant or have learned to suppress them or simply have fewer needs altogether.

The remarriages that are the most successful are the ones that know how to navigate difficult times while still being able to express their needs and have them met.

Healthy people are aware of their needs, respect them, and know how to appropriately get those needs met. It's why we marry each other—because we think our spouse can meet our needs even if those needs are not always clearly defined. For example, some temperaments have a great need for socialization, affection, and affirmation. When they do not have enough relational connection, life feels unfulfilling, and they may become depressed, feel rejected, or act out.

Other temperaments need quiet and solitude, but if they lack the necessary alone time to process, study, or reflect, they withdraw from others, disconnect, and may become easily annoyed. Some temperaments are independent and do not want anyone to tell them what to do or how to do it. Others are distinctly dependent and pursue input from others to help them make decisions and receive guidance, and they tend to focus on pleasing others.

The provided examples illustrate a critical principle: unmet needs lead to serious issues. They create conflict, disappointment, disillusionment, despair, and sometimes depression. And at the heart of most arguments is an unmet need. For whatever reason, shortly after the honeymoon—or even during the honeymoon period—so many married couples seem to forget the importance of meeting each other's needs. Without intervention, the couple risks emotional detachment and may seek to meet their needs in ways that are inappropriate or harmful to the relationship.

Consider this case study. Bill's temperament requires a high need for socialization, and he is naturally talkative. This talking, which often involves a lot of details, can feel tedious, even overwhelming, for his wife, Sue. While dating, Sue patiently listened with the hope that Bill would eventually slow down and talk less and with less intensity.

She likes the quiet and can sit in the same room with him and enjoy his company without saying a word. At times, she feels like Bill is insensitive to her need for quieter, less verbal connection.

As time goes on, Bill's need for communication escalates, which is the opposite of what Sue had hoped for. Her tolerance diminishes, and she becomes less patient and more irritable. Bill, confused by her behavior, becomes more aggressive. He wants to talk with her about what is going on. Sue withdraws more. Bill pursues more. Eventually, this couple becomes emotionally detached from one another, and by the time they're sitting in our office, their communication has degenerated along with their social life and affection.

Our work, then, was to help them develop a better understanding of each other's needs and show them how to meet those needs, recognizing that both sets of needs, different as they may be, are real and legitimate and were given to them by God. This gave them a renewed sense of hope and provided the tools and encouragement to work toward a compromise so that they could both meet each other's needs.

We write about temperament analysis because we've worked with thousands of couples and families who found a simple yet powerful tool that strengthened their bonds by allowing them to understand and meet each other's needs.

Take Action

The Arno Profile System is available in versions for adults, teens, and children, but it is not a self-assessment tool. To truly understand and use the profile, you will need the help of a trained temperament therapist. Visit the National Christian Counselors Association website for information on how to find a temperament therapist near you.

Lord Jesus, help us better understand each other through the lens of temperament. Help us identify both our negotiable and nonnegotiable needs so that we can foster a loving, compassionate, understanding, and fulfilling relationship as the people God created us to be.

21

Practicing Communication

Understand this, my dear brothers and sisters:
You must all be quick to listen, slow to speak, and slow to get angry.
JAMES 1:19 NLT

Good verbal communication is essential to virtually every relationship, and remarriage is no exception. Daily life comes with so many moving parts that if we don't communicate well, then those parts quickly begin to fall through the cracks, causing even more problems.

Thankfully, so many of the informational pieces of daily life can now be handled by an email or a short text: "A quick reminder that you said you could pick up Sara from school today. I appreciate it." Having a shared calendar for everyone to see, whether it's handwritten or on an app, can also help keep track of moving parts.

A couple's communication, however, must go beyond the sharing of basic information. In order to maintain closeness and connectedness with our partners, we need to share on the "feeling" level. For example, Ron once suggested that we share how we felt about our day instead of sharing all the details of what happened: "I felt needed and useful today...I felt overwhelmed and unproductive...I felt betrayed by my closest coworker."

Sharing our feelings with our partner often leads to a bigger discussion about what lies behind those feelings, which helps us better understand and help one another. If you disagree with something your partner says, you can be honest with them but remember to "speak the truth in love" (Ephesians 4:15 NLT).

We must also stress the importance of making sure your partner feels heard when sharing. We all want to know that our partners are truly listening when we speak, and not only to what we say but also to what we *don't* say. That's why it's important to listen to our partners' tone, watch their body language, and understand their present circumstances. When we do, we can ask appropriate, relevant, helpful questions that encourage them to express themselves even more. When we feel heard and understood, we are more likely to trust our partner, share more in the future, and connect on an even deeper level.

When we feel heard and understood, we are more likely to trust our partner, share more in the future, and connect on an even deeper level.

A sure way to make our partners feel heard and seen is to give them our undivided attention. Multitasking while supposedly listening sends the message that our partner doesn't deserve our full attention and that whatever task we're doing is equally as important as they are, which is never the case since our partners are the most important people in our lives. We don't want to take them for granted or neglect them, both of which can lead to a breakdown in the marriage. It is our presence and undivided attention that are perhaps the best gifts we can give to one another. So put the phone down, stop unloading the dishwasher or folding the laundry, and practice active listening.

Take Action

Share with each other one thing that you try to do to help your partner open up and one thing that you need from your partner in order to be more open. Assess the quality of your current communication by answering the following questions and then share your responses with your partner.

- Do we give each other our full, undivided attention?
- Do we focus on what's positive?
- When we share our feelings, do we talk more about ourselves or our partner?
- Do we avoid criticizing or blaming?

Father, teach us to speak honestly with love and to listen humbly. Help us remember to take the time to be truly present with each other and share our true feelings so that we can connect with our hearts. Amen.

22

Nurturing Intimacy

"At last!" the man exclaimed. "This one is bone from my bone, and flesh from my flesh! She will be called 'woman,' because she was taken from 'man.'" This explains why a man leaves his father and mother and is joined to his wife, and the two are united into one.

GENESIS 2:23–24 NLT

We all have an innate desire to be intimately connected to another person. To be known by another and to truly know another. We long for emotional, physical, and spiritual oneness, and it's what each of us hopes to find in a lifelong partner, even if we express it differently. To meet this person is to find our "soulmate," and it is a blessing to find one to accompany us through life.

Perhaps we unknowingly expected to find our soulmate in our first marriage but didn't. Perhaps we ourselves were not ready or able to be a soulmate to our first spouse. In the remarriage, blended-family journey, we get a second chance to be that person for someone else and for them to be that person for us.

To be someone's soulmate means that we are intimately connected to our partner in every way. Soulmates are there for one another and feel free to express their feelings, needs, anxieties, innermost thoughts, and faith in God without fear of rejection or judgment. When we have a soulmate, we know that we can freely express those things to that person at any given time, day or night. It's called emotional accessibility.

Emotional accessibility is one of the most important prerequisites to being someone's soulmate. It's like being "on call' for each other at all times. To be emotionally accessible means that we can connect with our partner on a deep level almost instantaneously. We have immediate access to each other's thoughts, feelings, and prayers, and we know that we can get our spouse's undivided attention any time that we may need it (within reason, of course). By making ourselves emotionally accessible to our partner, we nurture our emotional intimacy and strengthen our connection.

**By making ourselves emotionally accessible
to our partner, we nurture our emotional intimacy
and strengthen our connection.**

Another way that couples express their closeness and emotional intimacy is through sexual intimacy. In the same way that soulmates have emotional accessibility to one another, married soulmates also need sexual accessibility to each other, assuming no medical or physical reason prevents it. Sexual intimacy is another one of those amazing gifts that God gives to married people. It serves as one of the many ways that a couple can express the love and depth of their relationship.

If sexual intimacy isn't present, it may be related to past violations or damaging sexual experiences. A couple must work through these challenges so that intimacy can flow freely in the remarriage. Another obstacle that a couple may need to work through is the fact that remarried partners have already shared sexual intimacy with another person. Spouses will need to openly and honestly discuss the feelings associated with this reality, or it may persist as an obstacle.

Take Action

Share with your partner your responses to the questions and prompts below.

1. How do you feel about the fact that I have already been physically intimate with another person?
2. When I talk about sex, I feel...
3. One thing that worries me about sex is...
4. One thing that I find sexually attractive about you is...
5. How often would you like to be physically intimate?

Loving Father, you desire for us to be one with you. Like the oneness between you and your Son or you and your church, you have given us the gift of being one with our spouse. May we honor you and honor each other in all ways every day with your help.

23

Working through Conflict

Be completely humble and gentle;
be patient, bearing with one another in love.
Make every effort to keep the unity of the Spirit
through the bond of peace.

EPHESIANS 4:2–3 NIV

Conflict is inevitable in any close relationship. And in the case of the blended family, everyone has different temperaments, different backgrounds, and different experiences. Our basic values may be the same, but beyond that, we all have our own perspectives of life, marriage, and family. No two people will think, feel, or behave exactly alike, nor should that be the goal of a healthy marriage.

Because conflict in a marriage is inevitable, it is critical for couples to know how to navigate it. Healthy couples deal with conflict directly. Some couples even set aside time to "argue" or discuss differences and seek resolutions. In this chapter, we'll share simple, tried-and-true principles for addressing and moving through conflict.

The first step in any conflict is to share what you think and feel. We can't assume that our partner is a mind reader who knows our thoughts and feelings, nor should we assume that we know what our partner is thinking and feeling. Tell your partner what's bothering or upsetting you. Be honest and "speak the truth in love" (Ephesians 4:15 NLT). That means keeping the volume down, staying calm, and using a respectful tone.

Here's an example of what that could sound like: "If I seem frustrated or angry, it is because I waited forty minutes for you after you promised to be on time. I know you can get caught up in what you are doing, but I have a lot to do today as well. Waiting for you makes me feel like you don't respect me or my time." Respecting one another is essential, and appreciating your differences is healthy and nourishes the relationship.

Keep the conflict simple. That is, try to limit the conversation to one singular conflict that you can both identify and acknowledge as the present issue. Don't bring up old arguments or delve into the entire history of your relationship. Slow down and focus on the issue that's affecting you today so that your spouse does not feel overwhelmed, defensive, or resentful because you are hanging on to events of the past that he or she thought were already resolved. Allowing the disagreement to go "global" complicates the discussion and prevents you from solving the conflict at hand.

Sometimes, the best thing you and your partner can do is simply agree to disagree. Not everything is worth the conflict, so choose which battles are worth fighting and which ones are not. Keep things in perspective by asking yourself if this conflict will matter one year from now, ten years from now, or even next week. If it will matter in the future, then be willing to negotiate and compromise and remain solution oriented. If what you wish to say will not contribute to a solution or a compromise, then it's probably best left unsaid.

If what you wish to say will not contribute to a solution or a compromise, then it's probably best left unsaid.

It's tempting to resort to fighting when our emotions boil over. But fighting for the sake of fighting is unproductive and poses several risks to the relationship, such as breeding resentment, saying hurtful things, and placing undue stress on the relationship, to name just a few.

When emotions start to run high, consider revisiting the issue later, once both of you have had time to calm down and gain perspective.

In the midst of conflict, prayerfully recall the positive and joyful experiences you have shared together—if you can. Easier said than done. Without denying the present conflict, look toward the bigger picture, the long term. Keep your eyes on Jesus, "the champion who initiates and perfects our faith" (Hebrews 12:2 NLT).

What matters most—always—is honoring and preserving the unity that God has given to us. We must learn to appreciate, accept, and respect the great promise that nothing can separate us from the love of God. There will be times when we will not like our spouse or their behavior, which comes and goes. But true love is steadfast. It never changes.

Take Action

Agree on a time when you are both willing to calmly work on a conflict. Identify the conflict and write it down so that you are both in agreement about what you need to address. Ask God to help the two of you come to an agreement without hurting one another. Develop a strategy to try to resolve the conflict. If that strategy doesn't work, reassess and be prepared to try a new approach.

Lord, help us to be humble, gentle, and patient with one another. We may not always agree, but we know you want us to enjoy the peace and unity that you offer through your Spirit. Remind us of this gift and help us to accept and appreciate it.

24

Addressing Legal Matters

Keep your lives free from the love of money
and be content with what you have, because God has said,
"Never will I leave you; never will I forsake you."
HEBREWS 13:5 NIV

It may not be the most romantic notion, but remarrying comes with serious legal matters to consider. Will you prepare a new will? If so, to whom do your assets go? Will there be name changes for you or your spouse? How will you file your taxes? What will happen to your retirement accounts? Whose attorney will you see? Will you have a prenuptial agreement?

It may not be the most romantic notion, but remarrying comes with serious legal matters to consider.

Prenuptial agreements are much more common these days than they once were. So are divorces. And while a prenup can legally protect your assets in the event of another divorce, it can also do a great deal of emotional harm. Prenups, by nature, operate on the assumption that the marriage might not succeed. This can send a harmful message to your new partner that your assets are more important than the marriage itself.

Worse yet, a prenup puts in writing that you don't trust your spouse to handle your assets according to your wishes upon your death.

The hurt feelings caused by a prenup often go unspoken or unaddressed directly, but they can breed insecurity, which is never healthy.

You may think that everyone does or should do a prenuptial agreement, especially in a remarriage, but think twice about this. For a marriage to survive and thrive, both partners must be fully committed—for life. No loopholes. Whatever your decision may be, you'll need to discuss it together, giving each other the freedom to express opinions honestly.

In addition to considering prenups, there's also the matter of inheritance. As we discussed previously, a new couple must work out how all their children, both biological and step, will be provided for financially, including when one parent dies. It might surprise you to know that, despite the positive influence of a loving stepparent, the law does not grant any special status to stepparents as it relates to their stepchildren. The laws in every state set forth detailed provisions about each parent's rights and duties, but stepparents typically have very few, if any, rights with regard to their spouses' children.

When a parent dies, what are the stepparent's legal financial responsibilities to their stepchildren? Technically none. If a biological parent is concerned about his or her child's financial provision after the parent dies, then the parent must make a plan prior to or early in the remarriage. Perhaps that means establishing a trust fund in each child's name. Whatever arrangements the parent makes, the new spouse must be made aware of them.

If a stepparent wishes to leave part of the couple's estate to his or her stepchildren or divide the estate equally among both partners' children, then a will is essential. The specific wording is also critical since the words *children* or even *all my children* do not specifically include stepchildren, leaving the will subject to questioning or potential misinterpretation. Again, be as specific as possible.

There's also the matter of financial provision for the spouse who's left behind. We have known all too well of situations in which a long-time remarriage ended in the death of a partner whose biological children inherited all the assets of the estate, leaving the grieving second spouse with nothing.

While it is easy to assume that your second spouse will be taken care of upon your death, be sure that you clearly spell out all the details and that all parties understand, including adult children. Then make your decisions legal with the help of an attorney.

Although money and assets can be difficult topics to discuss, remember the unity and peace that God wants for you: "Make every effort to keep yourselves united in the Spirit, binding yourselves together with peace" (Ephesians 4:3 NLT).

Take Action

Have an open discussion with your partner about these two important questions: What is our plan for providing for all of our children if and when something happens to us, and what is our plan for providing for one another? Meet with an attorney to put your wishes in writing.

Loving Father, you desire to give us everything, including a wonderful inheritance with you forever in heaven. Help us sort out our feelings about our children and our stepchildren. Help us to look to your love and generosity as a model for our decisions.

25

Handling Finances

Teach those who are rich in this world not to be proud and not to trust
in their money, which is so unreliable. Their trust should be in God,
who richly gives us all we need for our enjoyment.

1 TIMOTHY 6:17 NLT

Like many divorced people, your divorce may have resulted in great
financial loss that forced you to make major lifestyle changes. You may
have had to return to work or take a second job to make ends meet or
pay child support. You may find yourself on your own with little to no
financial support from your former spouse. You may feel guilty that
you can no longer do things for your children that they were once
accustomed to. Your money and how you spend it inevitably change
not only after divorce but also when remarrying.

How a couple handles finances can unite or divide a family, so
when we prepare to remarry, it is imperative to discuss and evaluate
financial attitudes and expectations—well before the marriage. Honest
conversations about money may not be the most comfortable, but
they're critical. They prevent arguments and misunderstandings and
keep feelings of anger and resentment at bay.

The most important discussion for remarried couples to have
regarding money is how they will make financial decisions. Will the
spouses keep their money separate, or will they pool it into one shared
pot? Will he pay for his children and she pay for hers? Who's responsible
for purchasing everyday household items, like laundry detergent, paper
towels, and toilet paper? If one spouse assumes financial responsibility

for everyone, what feelings might this arrangement trigger in both partners and the children?

The most important discussion for remarried couples to have regarding money is how they will make financial decisions.

Families who work out of a single pot without distinguishing between "yours and mine" exhibit a high level of trust and commitment. This results in strong family unity and positive attitudes. However, couples need to move at their own pace toward such arrangements and not feel guilty or pressured if they do not immediately, or ever, feel comfortable handling their finances in this way.

For example, individuals who experienced economic hardship as a result of their divorce may feel the need to maintain control over their money in order to feel secure. This insistence for financial independence, however, can come at the cost of setting a negative tone with a new spouse and his or her children. Regardless, you and your new spouse will have to come to an agreement on how separate or blended your finances will be.

It's entirely normal to feel overwhelmed by the financial demands and responsibilities that come with marrying again and blending a family. Some people are still financially supporting or partially supporting their first family and worry about having to stretch their income between two households. Naturally, it's tough to accept some of these new realities without also feeling some resentment. We hear clients say things like,

Why do I have to support someone else's children?

What is his ex doing with all the support money we send? I never see it put toward the kids.

I'm tired of having to go without things because of how much my spouse is paying in support.

Be aware that these thoughts and feelings will likely come up at one point or another. Give your partner and yourself grace.

Another resentment that surfaces in remarriages is disparity in the treatment of the kids. We see this dilemma most when a former spouse spoils the children with events, trips, and material things that the stepsiblings do not also receive. We also see it when one parent holds expectations for their kids that the other parent does not have for theirs. For example, one parent may expect their kids to perform chores while the other kids have no such responsibility. Situations like this can divide the stepfamily and stir negative feelings among children, coparents, and new spouses. This dilemma will have to be addressed with the children and, if possible, the former spouse.

Although it feels unfair to the stepchildren, the reality is that the stepparent's former spouse might have the means to do more and buy more things than the stepparent. You will have to explain to the kids that while you wish you could do more, life is not always fair. It's a tough lesson for parents and kids alike, but remember that the most important things you can do for your children are to love them and spend quality time with them.

If you and your spouse are struggling with conversations about money, our best advice is to seek an attorney or financial planner sooner rather than later. Because of how common remarriages are now, most of these professionals have experience with these matters and can be quite helpful. Even financially competent people must understand that finances in a stepfamily have unique challenges not to be underestimated.

Take Action

If you are preparing to remarry or have already remarried but haven't had an open conversation about money, take the time now to address and discuss the following questions together and make decisions where possible.

1. Will we pool our money or keep it separate?
2. How will we pay household expenses, and who will handle paying the bills?
3. How much child support and/or spousal maintenance do you pay each month?
4. How much child support and/or spousal maintenance do you receive each month? If your former spouse does not make those payments, how will you provide for yourself and your children?
5. How will we handle expenses related to our children, such as childcare, activities, and medical bills?
6. What savings or investments do you possess?
7. What debts do you have?
8. Do you have life insurance? If so, how much does it cost each month, and who is the beneficiary? Do we need to make changes here?
9. Where will we live? If we move into a home owned by one of us, will we update the title on the home to include both names? Who inherits the house if one of us dies?
10. How do we feel about contributing toward the college education of each other's children?

Lord, money is a touchy and sometimes difficult subject for us to talk about. Help us be open and honest about all things related to our finances. We thank you for what you have provided for us and ask for your guidance in the areas in which we struggle.

26

Establishing Priorities

A man leaves his father and mother and is joined to his wife,
and the two are united into one.

GENESIS 2:24 NLT

First marriages usually begin with just the two spouses, allowing ample time and space to strengthen their bond and develop a shared lifestyle complete with their own routines and traditions. But in remarriage, at least one partner has already been married and brings a substantial amount of experience with them into the new marriage.

Remarriage requires couples to hit the ground running while trying to figure out how to bring together two separate lifestyles. For example, when one or both partners already have children, concerns of custody, former spouses, discipline, and finances loom large, robbing the new marriage of that critical "settling in" time. Or the partner without prior marital experience may feel that he or she is constantly living in the shadow of the partner's previous marriage.

In short, remarriages face many more challenges from the beginning than first marriages, so prioritizing the relationship of the married couple becomes more difficult. But the solidity of the marriage determines the stability of the stepfamily.

**The solidity of the marriage determines the stability
of the stepfamily.**

Many variables can separate a couple, and perhaps the most significant is the children. Because of our love for them, our guilt about the pain we may have caused them, our limited time with them, or our urge to prove our loyalty to them, it's natural and easy to prioritize the children above our new spouse, consciously or unconsciously.

Of course it's difficult to make it clear to our children that two seemingly contradictory statements are true at the same time: 1) Our spouse is now our first priority in our life, and 2) our love for them as our children remains the same. That is, we love them no less even though we've remarried and now prioritize the marital relationship. Children will not like this regardless of their age, but it is, nevertheless, the most important priority to establish. We'll expand more on the matter of loyalty in our next entry.

There is nothing that children of divorce need more than the assurance that *this* marriage will last forever and that they will not have to suffer the agony of another divorce. They need a sense of stability and confidence, and this will only come from making your new spouse your highest priority, as difficult and disloyal as it may feel. As it's been said, "The best thing you can do for your children is to love each other."[10]

Take Action

Assess how you are doing in the following critical areas:

- Spending quality time together
- Talking and sharing openly and honestly
- Listening with undivided attention
- Having fun
- Initiating romantic gestures
- Sharing intimacy
- Offering and receiving affection

Loving God, it is your plan that we live in marriage as one. Help us demonstrate to those around us, especially our children, that the gift of marriage that you have blessed us with is our top priority. Thank you for giving us the capacity to have plenty of love to go around. May your unfailing love surround and encompass our new family.

27

Competing Loyalties

"Those who come to me cannot be my disciples unless they love me more than they love father and mother, wife and children, brothers and sisters, and themselves as well...In the same way," concluded Jesus, "none of you can be my disciple unless you give up everything you have."

LUKE 14:26, 33 GNT

When two people get married, they each expect their spouse to be faithful and loyal to them first and foremost. They express this marital loyalty in a deep, lifelong commitment that transcends loyalty to friends and family. In a remarriage, loyalty can be tested to the max, especially when children are involved.

Strong feelings of loyalty to one's own children often come as a surprise to those beginning to blend families. Loyalty issues, however, are often a big source of unidentified conflict. In other words, people do not always recognize conflicts of loyalty for what they are. But in blended families, matters of loyalty are complex.

Much as we think we love our new spouse, we may quickly discover that when push comes to shove, our loyalty lies with our children. Below are some of the recurring comments we hear from clients, both adults and kids.

> My children can be out of line at times, but when he points it out or corrects my kids, I feel my loyalty rise up in their defense even when I know that what he is saying is the truth.

Sometimes it feels like her former spouse has more say in our plans than I do.

How will my mom feel if I enjoy doing things with my stepmom?

Ever since she came into the picture, I never get alone time with my dad anymore. He always wants to do things with her.

If I tell Mom what Dad let me do, then she'll think he's a bad parent.

These loyalty struggles are normal dynamics of blended families, and, like every other challenge, they take time to work through. Letting children know that what they're feeling is normal and that you understand will help them remain open to expressing themselves. Put their minds at ease by reminding them that enjoying time with their stepparent does not mean that they love their biological parent any less.

Adults, too, need to express their feelings honestly and respectfully. Here's an example of what that might sound like: "When you side with your kids against me, it undermines my role as their stepmom and makes me feel like an outsider. I am afraid that your kids will never accept or respect me." As we have said throughout this book and in the previous chapter, the couple's relationship must come first. Talk together about decisions related to the children.

Ultimately, loyalty goes back to our priorities. We are most loyal to what we're most committed to, and we're most committed to the things that we devote our time and energy to. If we want our stepfamily to come together and thrive, then we must make it a priority.

We are most loyal to what we're most committed to, and we're most committed to the things that we devote our time and energy to.

It is indeed difficult, uncomfortable, and in some ways painful to set aside strong loyalties in favor of new loyalties, but it is necessary work that we must all do. The good news is that as we learn to recognize our loyalties, we become more aware and more conscientious of how our actions affect our blended family.

In the much bigger picture, Jesus reminds us that we must love him more than we love anyone else. Doing this is the ultimate loyalty challenge that promises the ultimate rewards: the gift of an eternal relationship with him and an abundant life here and now.

Take Action

Rate the following priorities in order from one to seven, with one being your highest priority.

- Myself
- My relationship with my partner
- My children
- God
- My friends
- My career
- My hobby

My instinct is to side with my kids, Lord. Help me make my relationship with my spouse my priority while letting my kids know that I will always love them. Make my loyalty first to you, then to my spouse, and then to our kids, in that order.

28

Children's Feelings

> "I know the plans I have for you," declares the Lord, "plans to prosper
> you and not to harm you, plans to give you hope and a future."
> JEREMIAH 29:11 NIV

The feelings of children of divorce can often get lost in the shuffle. It's arguable that they are, in fact, the ones who suffer most. They experience many of the same emotions as the adults, but they might not be capable of expressing or coping with them. Let's try to better understand some of the common challenging emotions that they experience so that we're better equipped to provide the love, care, and attention they need.

Children have no choice in their parents' decision to get a divorce or remarry. That's why it's sometimes said that the biggest loss for children is that of control. That is, they lose control over the life that they've known and what they can expect from it. They may have to move geographically, which comes with the loss of familiarity, such as their home, neighborhood, school, or friends. Financial changes may create other losses, such as a change in lifestyle. For example, a parent may no longer be able to afford the same sports and activities that their child has enjoyed. Many children will lose daily contact with one of their parents too.

Sometimes, just as children begin to adjust to life in a single-parent home and to appreciate the extra closeness and attention of the one parent, the threat of remarriage comes along and presents yet another new set of circumstances. A remarriage means that children must now learn to share a parent with another adult and sometimes other children, forcing them to confront the loss of the common, secret fantasy that their parents will someday reconcile.

Take time to talk with and listen to your children. Give them an opportunity to share what they are feeling, noting that you may have to help them understand the concept of loss. Let them know that you understand because you, too, are feeling loss. But most importantly, stress that you know loss hurts and that you're aware that they may be feeling it. Tell them they might always feel this loss but assure them that things will get better in time.

Since children have no say in their parents' divorce, the lack of control they may feel can lead to acting out or expressions of anger toward one or both parents or toward a stepparent. If the remarriage forces them to change schools or homes, their anger may be directed primarily toward their custodial parent, the stepparent, or the parent they feel is most responsible for the divorce. Since family is the one thing that they thought they could always count on, it may take time for them to trust adults again, including their own parents.

Again, talking and listening are critical. Instead of reacting negatively to your children's angry behavior, give them an opportunity to express what they are angry about. The cause of their anger might be a complete surprise to you. Conversely, you may have to help them identify what has angered them, but don't put words in their mouths. Be a compassionate listener and tell them that you love them and understand their anger.

Some children blame themselves for their parents' divorce, believing that if they had been better behaved, then their parents might still be together. They might even punish themselves by insisting on quitting activities that they once loved or by spending less time with friends.

It may be difficult for us to talk about divorce, but answering their questions with age-appropriate responses helps to calm their fears and alleviate any guilt they might be feeling. Assure your children that they are not responsible for the divorce and that even though you and their other parent could not work things out, it does not mean that either of you loves them any less.

It is important to also remember that no matter how you may feel about your former spouse, he or she is still your child's parent. Your child has an innate love for them, and your former spouse has an innate love for your child. Avoid saying anything negative about your former spouse as this can sometimes prompt your child to become extra protective of that parent, and it may even lead to your child resenting you for it.

The responsibilities and expectations of a new marriage, stepchildren, or job may lead to you spending less time with your children than they're used to. Children may worry that their parent no longer loves them or that their parent cares more about their new spouse or the spouse's children than about them. All these factors can slow a child's acceptance of the new marriage.

Children also fear losing another family. It takes time for them to invest in a blended family. Conflict in the remarriage raises this fear again and again. This is why, when we counsel couples, we put such strong emphasis on prioritizing the relationship of the couple. The more stable and solid the children perceive the remarriage to be, the more secure they feel.

Constantly remind your children that you have plenty of love to go around, enough for everyone. Schedule individual time with each of them and make it happen. Your biological children need to know that they have not lost you to a new relationship, and your stepchildren need to see that you are serious about building a relationship with them.

The children who seem to cope best with all the changes of divorce and remarriage are the ones who are encouraged to maintain a good relationship with their other parent. A good relationship with both biological parents, even though the parents are not together, helps children continue to develop in healthy ways. In time, they will come to their own conclusions about each of their parents and let go of some of the feelings they experienced earlier in the process.

The remarriage of a parent (or both parents) can also bring hope. If children were living in a toxic, hostile, or abusive environment while their parents were together, they may now have hope that things will be better. An optimistic attitude about the future that is rooted in trusting God can bring hope to every member of the family. God has good plans for us, and we can trust that. Remind your kids of this too.

More than the things we buy for them, it is the time we spend with our children that touches them the most. Investing in our children and stepchildren is the greatest gift we can give them and yields lifelong rewards.

More than the things we buy for them, it is the time we spend with our children that touches them the most.

Take Action

Set aside regular time to check in with your children and stepchildren individually. Let them know you care for them and that they are safe to share their honest feelings—the good, the bad, and the ugly. Be open, understanding, and nonjudgmental. Ask God to help you give them all the support you can.

Lord, help me remember how my decisions affect my children. I know they have deep feelings, too, so help me to acknowledge them and support them each day, reminding them that you understand and love them. Help me to do the same.

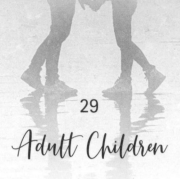

29

Adult Children

"The seeds that fell on the good soil represent honest,
good-hearted people who hear God's word, cling to it,
and patiently produce a huge harvest."

Luke 8:15 nlt

We sometimes hear couples say that their adult children will not be an issue in their remarriage because they are grown and have lives of their own. Let us assure you that this is an unrealistic attitude. In fact, adult children can make a remarriage much more difficult than young children.

We can neither assume that adult children will immediately be supportive of our decisions to remarry, nor can we expect them to not have concerns about it. Below we have shared real quotes from real adult children that indicate some of the feelings, thoughts, concerns, and attitudes that they experience.

> It was so great having Mom around to help with the kids. But now that Mom is in a relationship with him, she spends more time with his kids than mine.

> Now that Dad has remarried, I suppose that our inheritance will go to her.

> The least Mom could have done was wait awhile before marrying again. I have yet to get used to the idea that Mom and Dad are divorced and now this.

Since Mom's death, I have so appreciated the time with Dad alone. We were never so close, but now that she is in Dad's life, I never see him. They are so busy with their own lives. I feel like she has come between me and my dad.

We can neither assume that adult children will immediately be supportive of our decisions to remarry, nor can we expect them to not have concerns about it.

Even the people remarrying may feel torn about how their remarriage will affect their adult children. For example, consider the following quote from a remarried wife and her second husband, Tom.

Tom is so great about money. His attitude is that everything he has will be divided equally among his three sons and my two daughters. The problem is that I am not comfortable doing the same, and I feel guilty. My deceased husband worked so hard to set aside money for the girls' college funds. I feel disloyal giving some of that hard-earned money to Tom's sons.

We strongly advise couples to talk with adult children about plans to remarry. Ask them to share their honest feelings. Reassure them that you will still be there for them and that you're prepared to answer any questions or concerns they may have. Your decisions are still your own but be patient. In time, they will hopefully welcome your decision to remarry and express their happiness for you and your future.

Take it from us when we say that the good seeds you plant now with your children (of any age) will eventually produce a bountiful harvest. From the very beginning of our remarriage, Ron encouraged his young children to thank me, their stepmother, for the things I did for them. They diligently said thank you for the meals I cooked, the laundry I did, and the rides to school or to friends' homes.

At the time, I admit that I thought it might be a bit much and somewhat forced, but now that they're adults, his children continue to regularly express their appreciation to me. I receive cards, notes, and phone calls in which they thank me not only for the things that I do but also for just having been there all these years—and for still "being there" today.

Take Action

Schedule a time to talk with each of your adult children about your decision to remarry and how and why you decided on it. Listen to their feelings: happy for you, concerned, excited, angry. Ask them their reasons for feeling that way. Let them know that while this decision is yours to make, you still care about their feelings.

Lord, give me your guidance about how to talk and listen to my grown children about my remarriage. Give them understanding and wisdom as they share honestly with me.

30

Living Arrangements

"As for me and my household,
we will serve the Lord."

JOSHUA 24:15 NIV

The impact of housing decisions in remarriages is vastly underestimated. These decisions set the tone for the remarriage and the stepfamily. There are practical considerations, of course, such as whose home should be sold, whose home has the appropriate amount of space for the new family, or which home is in the desired area. Practical considerations, however, must not take precedence over the emotional needs of everyone involved.

Years ago, when we began our work with remarried couples, we would suggest beginning their life together by moving to a neutral location. After years of listening to blended families share their experiences, we now recommend definitively that remarried couples begin their life in a home that's new to everyone. This may not be the most logical decision from a financial perspective, but it's the best solution in so many other ways.

After years of listening to blended families share their experiences, we now recommend definitively that remarried couples begin their life in a home that's new to everyone.

Blending a family is an emotionally delicate process. And where a family chooses to live can be a positive, adventurous experience for remarried couples and their children. But if a remarried couple chooses to stay in one of their present homes and the new spouse moves into that home (with children), the potential for conflict is dangerously high.

That's why we suggest remarrying couples do their best to avoid what we call "land mines." A home that is filled with memories and nostalgia is perhaps the most subtle but potentially explosive land mine. Read on to hear from some of our clients' experiences with this.

When we got married, we decided to move into Dave's house because it was so much bigger than my small house. Dave and I agreed that we would redo the house to make it feel more like "our" house, but that became a struggle. We argued about how to incorporate my things with his things. If his children expressed dismay at my changing anything from the way their mother had arranged it, Dave refused to make the changes. I could not even paint a room a different color, let alone move furniture. I became angry and resentful toward both Dave and his kids.

When my brother and I moved into Catherine's home with our dad, I felt as though I was in a foreign land. I was still dealing with my parents' divorce (and not well, I might add), and now had to accept the fact that I had also lost my home, my room, my neighborhood, and my school. Catherine and her children made it clear that this was "their" house. They had their way of doing things, and there were a million unspoken expectations for us. Since we did not know what they were, we were constantly "making trouble" without even realizing it. Catherine was always upset with my brother and me and also our dad because we were not doing things "her way." It seemed to us that her kids got all the privileges and we were just there to do all the chores. I resented her and lost all respect for my dad for not standing up for us.

When Ron and I got married, we could not afford much, but our new home together was home to all of us right from the start. We all talked about respecting each other's space and things. We shared in the chores, and we created new ways of doing things together. We had family meetings to discuss problems before they got out of hand and began new traditions together. Most importantly, we all moved into our new home together. It was one of the best decisions we've ever made.

Take Action

Talk with your partner after reading this section and share possible solutions that consider everyone's feeling of belonging. If you are not yet living together, discuss how you can start a home in a space that's new to everyone. If you are already living in a home that previously belonged to one of you, have a serious discussion about moving into a new home. Then plan and work together to make the new space home to all.

Lord, give us guidance about our housing situation. Although this seems like a simple, basic need, we understand its significance. We know that, with your help, we can find the best solution for everyone.

31

Blended Family Feelings

"Don't sin by letting anger control you."
Don't let the sun go down while you are still angry,
for anger gives a foothold to the devil.
EPHESIANS 4:26–27 NLT

If we've learned anything so far, it's that feelings have power. Many blended families are triggered by the unique circumstances and issues that confront them, and the feelings that arise can be uncomfortable to say the least.

In this chapter, we will look at some of the common feelings, both negative and positive, that blended families experience. We'll also share relatable stories from our clients to help you understand just how common these challenges are.

Anger

Feelings of anger are legitimate. You may sometimes feel angry at your new spouse. You may be angry with yourself. You could be angry at your circumstances. As one client told us,

> When it was just us, without the kids, our life was great. But whenever his kids came for the weekend, I felt like our relationship all but disappeared. Our whole life revolved around those kids until I began to resent them and expressed it. My anger toward my new husband grew as I questioned how much of a priority I really was to him.

The bottom line is that holding on to anger will not change the past or create a better future. If you need help working through it, revisit chapter 6.

Guilt

"How can I ever make up for the pain that I have caused my children and family? What right do I have to be happy again?" These are common expressions of guilt. Remember that God always forgives us when we turn to him and ask for his forgiveness. He does not expect us to carry the burden of guilt forever. And because Jesus does not condemn, there is no reason for you to condemn yourself or allow others to condemn you. Trust his promise. Revisit chapter 7 for more help dealing with guilt.

Loneliness

Change, conflict, and emotional separation often bring feelings of loneliness. That's why, in a blended family, we all need to be alert, sensitive, considerate, and passionately present for one another.

> When my kids went on a trip with their dad, I felt left out and lonely. I wanted to be with them. Even though I am very grateful for the life I now have, there are times when I still feel lonely.

> When my spouse is with her kids, even if I'm with them, I often feel like the third wheel. It's lonely.

Doubt

When the going gets tough in any situation, it's natural to doubt your decision, especially in a blended family, where the stakes are so high.

> The first time we had a major blowup and his kids called me the wicked stepmother, I wondered what I had gotten myself into. I doubted my sanity and my discernment. Fortunately, with time, bringing my doubts to God in prayer and having ridden out these hard experiences, I eventually overcame my doubt.

Failure and Success

At times, we'll feel like a total failure as a spouse, parent, and stepparent. And rest assured, there will be tough, tough days. At other times, we feel successful or like we've mastered this thing called the blended family. We must remind ourselves that we're in a new, vulnerable position but also keep our eyes fixed on the horizon. What will things look like thirty years from now? That is the ultimate test of whether we have been a failure or a success.

Frustration

The very nature of a blended family is frustrating, and we might feel annoyed each day for many valid reasons. A blended family must establish how the household operates, and not everyone is going to seamlessly adjust.

> Before the kids leave for school every day, I am totally frustrated. Seldom does anything go like I planned. For a few hours each day, I get enough time to recoup and prepare for the next round of frustrating encounters.

A blended family must establish how the household operates, and not everyone is going to seamlessly adjust.

Gratitude

A remarriage presents an opportunity to be a positive influence in the life of a spouse and his or her children and to reenergize everyone with hope for the future. And if we keep making the investment, we will eventually receive the dividend and enjoy the fulfillment.

Take Action

Journal about which of these feelings you experience most often. Remember that all of them are common and normal, and most of them are temporary.

Loving and understanding God, each of these feelings can be overwhelming in and of itself. Help me to remember that they are normal and will pass with time, patience, and love—your love.

32

Between Two Households

May God, who gives this patience and encouragement,
help you live in complete harmony with each other,
as is fitting for followers of Christ Jesus.

ROMANS 15:5 NLT

When children spend time between Mom's house and Dad's house, they usually must cope with two different sets of values, beliefs, and lifestyles. Many of them must deal with new stepparents and stepsiblings as well. Adjusting is bound to be difficult.

In our experience, and that of most blended families, there are periods of transition when kids arrive at one home and prepare to return to the other parent's home. Transitions are difficult for kids (and adults). Having to travel between two homes is a stark reminder that their biological parents are indeed divorced. Subconsciously, kids must confront that hard, painful truth every time they leave one home and arrive at the other, which can foster anxiety and elicit grief. Again, remaining aware of these feelings and learning how to respect them is essential.

To support our kids in the early hours of their return to our home, we gave them time to settle in and did not expect much from them in terms of conversation or participation. We avoided scheduling plans and events that would take place immediately upon their arrival, but when necessary, we forewarned them of what to expect and lowered our expectations of their enthusiasm.

On the other end of their stay, we kept things low key in their last few hours with us before returning to the other parent's home. We found that activities that pushed right up to the time they would have to leave caused stress and anxiety for all of us and made transitions even harder. Getting in tune with the rhythm of children coming in and going out of the home and remaining patient through these tough times will ease transitions and minimize unpleasant hellos and goodbyes.

Many parents also report feeling unprepared for the challenge of transporting things like clothes, stuffed animals, or bikes between households. Having to pass things back and forth from home to home is a burden on children and parents alike. The worry of forgetting important things, which happens sometimes, brings everyone stress and can cause feelings of anger over the divorce to resurface.

In an attempt to relieve some of the back-and-forth burden, we made sure that some of our kids' basic items stayed at our home. This sometimes meant purchasing doubles of special clothing, shoes, toiletries, toys, et cetera, but it was worth it. It alleviated the stress of having to remember everything and helped minimize feelings of resentment toward the other parent when certain items never returned to our house.

If purchasing doubles of items is not financially possible, then try providing your children with a list of what they might want to bring to your house. If you're going on a family bike ride, for example, you can list a bike as an item to bring. You can also include on the list basic but important items that they might forget, like their backpacks for school. Tell the children that you understand how hard it is for them to have to think through what they will need and that you hope the list will make it easier.

Another common frustration that comes with living between two homes is the difference in household values, attitudes, rules, and boundaries. It can be upsetting when your child says or does something that you consider unacceptable or inappropriate only to find out it's permitted or encouraged at the other parent's house: "Dad always lets us stay up late. Why do we have to go to bed so early over here?"

Acknowledge that things may be different at their other parent's home, without being critical, and tell them you understand that it's difficult to readjust. However, still assert that "this is how we do things here." This relays clear expectations to children, which is helpful even if they don't like it.

We went out of our way to explain to our kids where our beliefs and priorities came from and why we held them. They had to abide by our rules while they were with us, but we assured them that our motivations were to love and protect them.

As kids get older, it's common for them to resist traveling between households. As their lives get busier, they lack the time and energy to frequently make the transition. We struggled not to take it personally, and we increasingly permitted the kids to set their own schedule more and more—within reason. We also found new ways of spending time with them. Going out for coffee, lunch, or dinner together was easier. These special times often connected us more meaningfully than their transitioning to us for the weekend, only to spend most of their time with friends or at activities.

The takeaway here is to remain aware of the fact that living between two households is anything but easy for kids of any age. Letting them know that you understand the challenge and love having them with you is the best and most important thing we can do. Our job is to be sensitive, caring, compassionate, patient, and, of course, flexible. These are the keys to helping everyone handle all the moving parts that come with living between two homes.

Remain aware of the fact that living between two households is anything but easy for kids of any age. Letting them know that you understand the challenge and love having them with you is the best and most important thing we can do.

Take Action

Set up a time to talk with each of your children about what it's like having to travel back and forth between homes. Ask them what you can do to make things a bit easier for them and let them know that you and your new partner will do all that you can to help them. Then follow through with that promise.

God, you know better than we do what our kids deal with every day. Help us be sensitive and compassionate with them. Help us be flexible when necessary and unwavering when it's in their best interests.

33

School Support

They have been a wonderful encouragement to me, as they have been to you. You must show your appreciation to all who serve so well.

1 CORINTHIANS 16:18 NLT

When children travel back and forth between two households, it is their school that most often remains the same. In fact, school can be the most stable force in the life of a child whose parents are going through a divorce or remarrying. Because of this, parents should do their best to keep their kids in the school they're familiar with, if possible.

When parents make teachers aware of major changes going on in a child's life, most teachers will respond by helping the child through the adjustment period in whatever ways they can. But when teachers do not know that the family is going through a transition or the family does not know how to utilize the school's resources for support, children might feel like they're suffering alone, assuming they're the only kid in school going through such a hard time. They may very well feel confused or embarrassed: "None of the other kids have to live in two different houses and go back and forth. I hate it!"

Involving neutral professionals in your child's school system can go a long way in helping your kids deal with the changes and feelings related to the divorce or remarriage. For example, if a parent is in tremendous pain or turmoil during a period of transition, he or she may not have the emotional capacity or stability to be their child's best outlet for support. Kids are perceptive, and if they see their parent struggling, it can be uncomfortable for them to express their true feelings. Instead, they try to protect their hurting parent.

Involving neutral professionals in your child's school system can go a long way in helping your kids deal with the changes and feelings related to the divorce or remarriage.

According to some reports, half of all children in the United States will witness the end of their parents' marriage, and half of those children will go on to witness the divorce of a parent's second marriage.[11] School systems are aware of these statistics, and we are seeing progress in how they are serving the needs of these families.

Schools are now more sensitive about language, broadening family terms to include "family members" and "caregivers" as opposed to just "mom and dad." Many teachers are also prepared to schedule two separate parent-teacher conferences and keep both households informed of happenings at school, whether that's via email or sending home duplicates of important school announcements or information. It's not uncommon for one parent to be more organized than the other, which sometimes means that a child may not always have the materials he or she needs or is supposed to bring to school. Informed teachers are better prepared to accommodate this and be more empathetic and understanding.

Ultimately, it is the parents' responsibility to keep the school informed. We cannot expect educators to anticipate our needs, which is why we must be proactive about remaining in close communication with them, respectfully sharing our needs and our kids' needs. We pray that busy teachers can be gracious, supportive, and patient. We, too, need to be gracious and patient.

Take Action

If you haven't already, make an appointment with your child's teacher to discuss the changes your family is going through and develop strategies together to support your child. Share any concerns you may have so that your child's teachers can be alert and sensitive to them.

Patient God and Father, we thank you for the commitment of so many wonderful educators. We ask that you help them support our children in these times of transition. Help us be patient with them and them with us.

34

Effective Stepparenting

It is required that those who have been given a trust
must prove faithful.

1 CORINTHIANS 4:2 NIV

As stepparents, we have been given a trust—a massive, hugely important trust that we must nurture because, like it or not, we are models, mentors, servant leaders, and caregivers. Stepparenting doesn't come with a clear job description or a manual; it is a day-by-day, event-by-event role. This role is a remarkable privilege and opportunity to positively impact the lives of our new spouse's children. In this chapter, we'll share quick tips to help you get started in stepparenting effectively.

Be realistic. Don't expect to love someone else's children or have them love you instantly. The truth is that you probably will not love your stepchildren the same way that you love your own biological children, but that does not mean that you won't love them. This is natural and common and not something to feel guilty about. It takes time for love to grow.

Be vulnerable. Admitting to stepchildren that you have never been a stepparent before and that you're learning and doing the best you can is helpful and builds trust. Apologize to them when you say or do something out of line. Ask them how you are doing from their perspective and what you might do differently. If appropriate, work on making those changes.

Get to know them. Let your partner's child know that you are not trying to take the place of their mother or father but that you hope to build a good relationship with them. One of the best ways to do that is to spend time with each child. Invite them to ride along while you run an errand. Take them out to eat or show up at their games. Ask them about themselves, what they enjoy doing, and who their friends are. Show a genuine interest in their life and appropriately answer any questions they may have of you.

Earn respect. Respect is earned with stepchildren, not a given. When you are not a child's biological parent, you do not have the right to discipline, correct, or tell a child what to do or not do just because you are an adult who's now married to their parent. This is not to say that you do not deserve the same respect that any adult would expect from a child, but as a new stepparent, you must first build a relationship with a stepchild and earn their respect before you have the right to attempt to parent.

Respect is earned with stepchildren, not a given.

Avoid making negative comments. Respect both of your stepchildren's biological parents by not making negative comments about them in front of the children. No matter how badly that person behaves or even if he or she is not in the child's life at all, that person is still the parent, and the child's loyalty will be with the biological parent, not with you. Respecting the child's parent will help the child develop respect for you.

Encourage parental relationships. Assuming both parents are present and involved, encourage stepchildren to maintain good relationships with both of them. You may not always agree with the lifestyle or decisions of your spouse or your spouse's ex, but seldom (perhaps never) is it appropriate to say so in front of the kids. Learning to bite one's tongue is one of the major skills to develop for a healthy remarriage.

Defer discipline. Leave all discipline of a stepchild to their biological parent unless you have been given permission by the parent to do so. We will say more about discipline in our next chapter, but this is a good rule of thumb.

Support your spouse. A stepparent often has objectivity that the biological parent does not. Discussions between the two of you can be helpful if the parent is open to another perspective. These conversations, however, must take place without the children present or within earshot.

Maintain a united front. Children can be major contributors to the division between two people, and they might do so if they see you routinely disagree with each other. Couples will need to remain alert to arguments and conflicts that too often focus on issues related to the children. This could be an indication that the children have come between the two of you, which is symptomatic of a dynamic you need to address the moment you discover it.

Take Action

Spend time with each of your stepchildren individually, helping them get to know you and you get to know them. Be appropriately vulnerable with them about some of your own feelings.

Lord, you have given me the gift of stepchildren. Give me the guidance, patience, and courage to build strong, healthy relationships with each of them. Direct me as to what to say and what not to say and help us learn to respect each other.

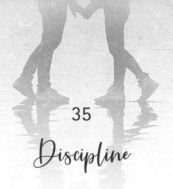

35

Discipline

My child, don't reject the Lord's discipline, and don't be upset when he corrects you. For the Lord corrects those he loves, just as a father corrects a child in whom he delights.

<small>PROVERBS 3:11–12 NLT</small>

All children need discipline, and we do it out of our love for them. And while the parenting skills needed to effectively discipline children are much the same for all families, discipline within stepfamilies looks a little different.

When biological parents discipline their children, the close bond they feel for each other helps the child more easily accept the parent's authority to set rules and boundaries. But in a stepfamily, stepchildren may resist or reject a new stepparent's attempts to discipline: "I don't have to obey you. You're not my mom/dad."

Until everyone has had time to adjust and develop close relationships with each other, it is best for each biological parent to discipline his or her own children. In the absence of the biological parent, however, the authority to discipline can be delegated temporarily to the stepparent if the arrangement is made crystal clear to the children. Even then, this right is reserved only for a designated period of time—while a sibling is getting picked up from an activity, while running and errand, or until the parent gets home from work, for example. If you receive this right, exercise it firmly, respectfully, and lovingly.

> **Until everyone has had time to adjust and develop close relationships with each other, it is best for each biological parent to discipline his or her own children.**

This arrangement works best when remarried couples share similar styles of discipline. You may not always agree on every single issue, but it's of the utmost importance that you consistently support each other. If the children complain to their biological parent about a stepparent's parenting while the parent was absent, then the biological parent must support the stepparent in front of the kids. If he or she disagrees with the stepparent or has questions about how a situation unfolded, the parent and stepparent must discuss it away from the kids to preserve the respect for the stepparent, not undermine it.

Most parents find discipline a challenge. It's to be expected that children will rebel and misbehave as they adjust to the blended family dynamic, but many behaviors are normal to childhood development.

In other words, not all bad behavior stems from living in a blended family. It will be necessary for remarried couples to develop a cooperative approach to discipline in order to provide a sense of stability and assert household boundaries, which children desperately need, particularly during times of transition.

Take Action

Away from the children, answer the questions below with your partner.

- What is my style of discipline? What is yours?
- What expectations do we have regarding the stepparent's approach to discipline?
- If we differ on how best to approach a conflict or situation, how will we address it so that we present a united front to the kids?
- Who will have the primary responsibility for the children?
- How will we set up our disciplinary structure?

Lord, it is not easy to know how best to discipline children, especially when they are not my own. Help me to remember that you discipline us out of your great love for us. I want to work at this challenge because of my love for them.

36

Incorporating Extended Family

The people who lived there were very good to us...
and welcomed all of us.
ACTS 28:2 NCV

Three of our six grandchildren have three sets of grandparents. Yep. Three grandfathers and three grandmothers, all of whom are active in their lives. Needless to say, the grandkids are sometimes confused about how and where all these grandparents fit into the family. Fortunately, everyone involved is gracious, so it works out. But it has not always been this way.

When we married, both of our parents struggled to accept our remarriage. For me, Nancy, our stepfamily was the first on my side of the family. The first Christmas after our wedding, my parents invited my two sons and me for dinner but not Ron and his children, saying they did not feel ready. I made the tough decision to decline their invitation, which made it the first Christmas that my sons and I did not spend with my family. I told my parents that even though I knew the changes were difficult, Ron and his three children were my family now. We came as a package deal. Fortunately, from that point on, we were all invited, and although it took quite a few years for everyone to feel comfortable, it did happen in time.

Our extended family is just a microcosm of what remarried couples and blended families can look like and experience. The reality is that family structures come in all shapes and sizes, which makes the process of incorporating extended family a bumpy ride at times. In this chapter, we'll share advice on how to integrate a blended family with extended family.

Prepare kids for meeting new people by explaining who they are in relationship to you. You might even consider drawing a family tree for them before meeting. Do the integration slowly, one or two family members at a time, if possible, and perhaps at your home, where the kids are in a familiar setting. These smaller meetings are helpful for integrating both the children and the family members before big events, like weddings or holidays. Large gatherings of unfamiliar people can overwhelm the kids and make them feel uncomfortable or like outsiders.

Prepare kids for meeting new people by explaining who they are in relationship to you.

When there is an appropriate moment, politely, briefly, and respectfully share with the relatives your requests about being cautious in their conversations with the kids when it comes to topics such as former spouses, the divorce, the new blended family, et cetera. These topics are often deeply personal, even for adults, and can make kids uncomfortable.

Our clients often ask us whether they should incorporate ex-spouses into the extended family. We have seen this done many times, but we don't recommend it. If you get along with your former spouse, that's wonderful, but including them in celebrations, such as kids' birthday parties or gatherings hosted at your home, can be confusing, especially to young children. It is difficult for them to make sense of where their other parent fits within your new family structure.

As we've mentioned before, most children, no matter their age, carry a secret hope that their parents will get back together, so seeing you together at family events can be misleading. It makes their hope for reconciliation seem realistic when it's not, which is unfair to them.

It is best when divorced couples can get along and work together in all instances for the sake of the children's best interest, but you and your ex lead separate lives now. There will be plenty of events where you will both be present to support your children, such as graduations, recitals, conferences, and sporting events. These events are inevitable, so it's important to be able to get along with your ex.

Take Action

Create a simple family tree that includes only the closest family members whom the children are most likely to see. Share pictures of relatives and mention a few of their positive characteristics or hobbies they might share in common with the kids. For example, if Uncle Fred likes to fish and so does your child, highlight that connection.

Lord, we know it can be difficult for everyone to feel comfortable meeting and integrating new people into a family. Help everyone involved to be gracious and welcoming. Give us all the patience to learn to accept one another as family.

37

Having an "Ours" Baby

Children are a gift from the Lord;
they are a reward from him.
PSALM 127:3 NLT

We frequently counsel remarried couples who have children from their previous marriage about the decision to have another baby, one that they can call "ours." The prospect of a new baby is exciting. After all, a baby is a physical embodiment of the love between two people. However, the decision to add a baby to a blended family is a monumental one, and it permanently impacts everyone in the household.

The decision to have another baby requires parents to take a great many things into consideration: Are we ready and/or willing to subject the children to more change? How might the children feel about a new sibling? Can we realistically afford another child? How might the new child feel when their half-siblings return to their other parents' homes and vice versa?

One of the first things for partners to discuss when considering a new baby is expectations. Partners who enter a remarriage without children may very well have expectations about the joy and excitement of finally becoming a parent, while a partner who already has children may be finished having children, having never considered the possibility of another baby or babies. Discussing the pros and cons together and seeking God's guidance is critical before making a decision.

A new baby can be the link that bonds everyone together, thereby strengthening the stepfamily: "In playing with, taking care of and talking to the baby, children can have something to share with an adult with whom they might otherwise feel they have nothing in common."[12] A new baby can also unite stepsiblings since a new baby is "new" to everyone.

On the other hand, a new baby can just as easily (and arguably more easily) divide a blended family. The children, having already been through their parents' divorce and remarriage, may still be adjusting to their new life and might not welcome another major life change. The children may feel jealous over the attention the baby will receive or insecure about getting even less time with you. They may wonder if you will still love them the same once there is a new baby to love. They may worry about practical concerns, like where the baby will sleep and if they'll have to share their room, or they may feel scared or resentful of the change.

Take Jill and Sam for example. Jill had never been married or had children when she met Sam, who had three sons from his previous marriage. Jill vowed to love his boys as if they were her own, a "vow" we frequently hear. But a year and a half later, when Jill and Sam had a son of their own, Jill began to realize that she did not love the older boys like she loved her own biological son. This made her feel guilty and uncomfortable around Sam's sons, who began to feel second best.

The boys' jealousy toward the new baby grew, and their resentment toward Jill made things even worse. Jill started taking trips with the baby to her mother's house on weekends when Sam's boys would be home. The new baby was a source of division in the family, leaving Sam and his boys on one side and Jill and the new baby on the other. Unfortunately, in their situation, the division was so powerful that it eventually ended their marriage.

Ideally, a couple should make the decision to have another baby, or at least discuss their openness to it, well in advance of the remarriage and probably during those initial dates when sharing hopes and plans for the future.

> A couple should make the decision to have another baby,
> or at least discuss their openness to it, well in advance
> of the remarriage.

However, there may also be value in taking the temperature of the current state of the home and resting in it before making a final decision. Regardless, if you and your spouse are contemplating adding another baby to your existing blended family, we urge you to take your time in making this decision, considering all the complexities and challenges that a new baby will bring to everyone's lives.

Take Action

Discuss with your spouse your present family dynamics and honestly share your thoughts, feelings, and concerns about potentially having another child. Pray together for God's direction rather than your own. Remember that God's plans for our lives are to bless us and not harm us.

Lord Jesus, help us put our trust in you for the complex decisions that we need to make that affect all of us. Help us set aside our own desires to listen to your plan for our lives and then to trust it.

38

Bringing Baby Home

Let us consider how we may spur one another on toward love and good deeds, not giving up meeting together...but encouraging one another.

HEBREWS 10:24–25 NIV

If you and your partner have decided to have another baby, or if God has surprised you with another baby, let us congratulate you! Whether you're feeling excited, anxious, or overwhelmed, rest assured that there is plenty that you and your spouse can do to prepare your children for the new addition and help them embrace their growing family.

You and your spouse will want to share with your children ahead of time your decision to have another baby, whether that's once you've made the decision to have a baby or once you are expecting. Whenever you decide to share the news with them, make the announcement a happy one of excitement and gratitude. Share with them your hopes for the family and your confidence in them as older siblings. If this gift of another baby was a surprise from God, then it should be announced as precisely that, followed by a discussion about everyone's honest feelings about it.

At this early stage, don't expect children to know their feelings yet, but plan on maintaining an ongoing dialogue throughout the pregnancy not only as a family but also individually with each child. Designate time for you to truly listen to them, particularly their fears. Let them know that you understand their concerns and that they are not bad or wrong for having them. Invite questions. Reassure them that a new baby can bring them joy and does not change your love for them in any way.

Involve the children throughout the pregnancy as much as possible. This will help them feel included and important and will help them begin to think beyond themselves as part of something bigger. Share with them the positive parts of having a sibling: a tiny one to love, cuddle, care for, teach, watch grow, and have fun with. With younger kids, read children's books about bringing home a new baby. Let them pick out toys and baby clothes, help set up the nursery, or learn how to change a diaper if they're old enough. Share ultrasound photos as the baby grows.

Once the new baby arrives, try to preserve the existing home routine as much as possible. Check in often with the kids to see how they're feeling. Show younger kids how to interact and play safely with the baby, and let older kids hold the baby, feed the baby, or change the baby's diaper. Praise the kids for their help and love. Consider using "brother" or "sister" instead of "half-brother" or "half-sister." Take family pictures of everyone together and hang them up throughout the house. Do things as an entire family, like eating dinner, watching movies, playing games, or attending fun events.

Again, keep an open dialogue and pay close attention to how the kids react to the baby's presence. Are they sighing or rolling their eyes when the baby comes up in conversation? Do they complain about helping to care for the baby? Their reactions will clue you in to how they're feeling. That's why the one-on-one time with each child is so important.

**Keep an open dialogue and pay close attention
to how the kids react to the baby's presence.**

You will need to work together as a couple to free up time for each of you to spend time with the children individually, preferably away from the busyness at home. Remaining proactive about spending this time together is invaluable and avoids the risk of children feeling newly displaced, which is sometimes a feeling that never goes away.

In all things, remain encouraging and continue to work on building a loving home. Go into this change knowing that there will be plenty of bumps and missteps along the way. Have grace for one another, pray together, and thank God for the gift of a growing family.

Take Action

Create a specific plan for how you will spend one-on-one time with each child and away from the new baby. Plan at least one simple, weekly family event to bring everyone together, including baby.

Thank you, Lord, for the gift of life. Thank you for the gift of this child and for all of our children. Unite us as a family that has received a new gift. Help us make everyone feel loved and valued, and guide us each day.

39

New Beginnings

"Forget the former things; do not dwell on the past. See, I am doing
a new thing! Now it springs up; do you not perceive it? I am making
a way in the wilderness and streams in the wasteland."

Isaiah 43:18–19 NIV

Scripture is meant to lead, guide, teach, encourage, protect, and comfort us. In this passage, Isaiah gives us important and practical advice as it relates to our remarriage: forget the former things. If we don't let go of the past, we risk getting stuck there, paralyzed by feelings of remorse, rejection, guilt, fear, anger, and loneliness. As Paul said, "If anyone is in Christ, the new creation has come: The old has gone, the new is here! All this is from God, who reconciled us to himself through Christ" (2 Corinthians 5:17–18 NIV).

One of the best ways to move on from our former life is to create new traditions. For our family, the new traditions that we personally formed together early in our remarriage were the things that united us as the uniquely blended family that we were and still are today. These traditions had not been a part of either of our families in the previous marriages.

**One of the best ways to move on from our former life
is to create new traditions.**

For example, we took several short trips while our five children were young. These trips gave the kids an opportunity to get to know each other better and learn how to have fun together. The experiences and locations of these vacations were new to all of us, so we experienced them for the first time together.

We started other family traditions, too, including a weekly family Bible study, family meetings, and Thanksgiving journals. These were journals in which each person in the family wrote a list of the things they were thankful for and a list of what they wanted the family to pray about for the coming year, and we'd share our lists. To this day, we pull out their notebooks at Thanksgiving, and we love reading and sharing past entries and adding new ones.

Father's Day and Mother's Day became opportune times for the kids to evaluate us in our roles. Even now that they're all adults, we still ask them to give us a grade each year. We repeat these and other activities, like stuffing Christmas stockings with small, practical gifts each year.

New traditions helped us all move forward together, shaping and molding a family life that was uniquely ours. It also helped us lean into all the good things that God prepared for us.

Before we leave this topic, we want to be clear about something. It may sound like we all died and went to heaven, where there is no more pain, suffering, sorrow, or tears. But the truth is that we all had our share of pain, suffering, sorrow, and tears. We all had moments of trauma and disappointment.

What we do know, however, is that with God's help, we made it through seriously challenging stuff. It's our belief that we made it through by following Scripture and praying—a lot. We did our best to open our hearts and eyes to embrace the new, wonderful work that God was and still is doing with and for us.

All seven of us (and now our children's spouses) are grateful for each other. Although some of us live in different parts of the country, our hearts and lives are bonded. We miss being together, and when we are together, we have fun and experience joy.

Take Action

Make a list of some of the amazing things that God has done to help you see more clearly how he orchestrated your coming together as a couple and as a blended family. Share the list with each other and thank God.

Thank you, Lord Jesus, for the powerful passage from the book of Isaiah and for the phenomenal gift of our blended family. Thank you for what you have done for each of us and what you will continue to do to help us embrace what you have prepared for our future.

40

Coparenting

[Jesus] did not retaliate when he was insulted, nor threaten
revenge when he suffered. He left his case in the hands of God,
who always judges fairly.

1 Peter 2:23 nlt

When a couple gets divorced, both individuals recalibrate their life-styles. Some celebrate their newfound independence and freedom. Others grieve the loss and reflect on what happened, perhaps even wishing they were still married. Some revisit college or adolescent behaviors. Sometimes their new lifestyle is so radically different from their previous one that former spouses become troubled by what they see, almost as if their former spouse has become unrecognizable or unpredictable. In these circumstances, differences emerge, and conflict magnifies.

Most of these conflicts center around the challenge of having to work together, be it for selling a home, dividing assets, establishing parenting time, determining where kids attend school, splitting costs for kids' expenses, et cetera. Whether we like it or not, we must learn how to navigate the new and often strenuous dynamic with our former spouse.

Decisions about kids require profound collaboration between parents, which can become complicated and contentious when parents differ in values, priorities, and parenting styles. Regardless of your differences with your former spouse, you should make all decisions with the needs of the children at the forefront. Major lifestyle changes have a substantial and sometimes permanent impact on children, which is why it's crucial to prioritize the kids' best interests and to minimize the number of changes in their life.

Regardless of your differences with your former spouse, you should make all decisions with the needs of the children at the forefront.

Amid the readjusting, some children inevitably become confused and conflicted. It's painful to accept, but kids who are hurting are vulnerable. Because they witness and experience their parents' struggles alongside them, they may seek other outlets in search of support. Unfortunately, some of those outlets lead to poor choices, such as forming friendships with others who may not be the best influence, isolating, or burying themselves in social media. Their schoolwork might suffer. Some will even turn to drugs or alcohol.

It's not uncommon for kids to pull away from both of their parents and share less openly (or not at all) about their life. For these reasons, we encourage parents to do their absolute best to rally together and set aside their differences for the sake of the kids. Hopefully other family members are available to listen and guide the kids through this transitional stage too.

Both parents will attend countless events throughout their children's lives. Think weddings, recitals, and graduations. And when parents can't get along or be cordial with one another, it's the kids who suffer. What should be an event celebrating the child becomes the stage for everyone to witness and experience the tension and discord between their parents. Not only can it be embarrassing and uncomfortable for the kids, but it can also sow seeds of resentment in their hearts and understandably so. Again, we must set aside personal differences and prioritize and respect the needs of the children first and foremost.

In the bigger picture, it can be helpful to remind ourselves that we were once married to our former spouse, and one of the blessings that came from that marriage is our children. Children need both parents, and we can ask God to help us do our very best to work together.

Risa Garon, author of *Stop! In the Name of Love for Your Children: A Guide to Healthy Divorce* and executive director of the National Family Resiliency Center, says, "Think of being a co-parent like being a business partner. This will take emotion out of the equation." She also suggests that parents agree to have short and respectful conversations and to refrain from blaming or judging each other when they speak.[13]

Consider this helpful advice from Saint Paul:

Dear brothers and sisters, one final thing. Fix your thoughts on what is true, and honorable, and right, and pure, and lovely, and admirable. Think about things that are excellent and worthy of praise. Keep putting into practice all you learned and received from me—everything you heard from me and saw me doing. Then the God of peace will be with you. (Philippians 4:8–9 NLT).

The quicker we can set aside our hurt and disillusionment from the divorce, find closure, and learn to take the high road, the quicker our relationship with and attitude toward our former spouse can heal and become a more productive, healthier one.

Take Action

Talk with your new partner about how you can support each other in difficult situations with former spouses. You may want to give each other permission to offer objective advice if you are both comfortable with that approach.

Lord Jesus, I know that I can do all things with the strength that you give me. Please cleanse me from my potentially negative attitude toward my former spouse so that my children can learn patience, acceptance, and respect from me.

41

Protecting Children from Adult Conflict

"Let the children come to me. Don't stop them! For the Kingdom of Heaven belongs to those who are like these children." And he placed his hands on their heads and blessed them.

MATTHEW 19:14–15 NLT

Meet the Andersons. The Andersons are a remarried couple who attended one of our blended family retreats before seeking couples counseling with us. They each had three children from their first marriages, and their post-divorce relationships with their former spouses remained contentious.

Hastened by financial pressures resulting from their respective divorces, the Andersons' remarriage and moving in together happened quickly. Both had been in and out of court with their former spouses several times within the first four years of being together, and their former spouses did everything they could to sabotage the remarriage—to the point where they had the kids write affidavits, which are legally documented statements, testifying to their negative feelings toward the remarriage. Involving kids in adult conflicts like this is a grave mistake.

We have worked with countless clients whose hearts and minds were permanently impacted as children from having regularly witnessed heated or hostile conflict between parents, divorced or not. These clients often carry detailed memories of their parents' arguments, and it's not uncommon for painful, uncomfortable, and unresolved feelings to emerge when they pursue romantic relationships of their own as adults. Consider the findings shared by the Institute for Family Studies, quoting research from *Parental Conflict: Outcomes and Interventions for Children and Families*:

> "Children from high-conflict homes are more likely to have poor interpersonal skills, problem solving abilities and social competence." Those problems negatively impact their romantic relationships in adolescence and adulthood, as conflicts cause children to "perceive themselves and their social worlds more negatively" and to "have more negative pictures or internal representations of family relationships." Thus the high-conflict relationship of one couple can produce other negative relationships in the next generation.[14]

As parents, we have a responsibility to protect our children from harsh realities and complicated conversations that kids are not yet ready to process or understand. While we value the thoughts, feelings, and opinions of our children, some conflicts, particularly those between adults, are inappropriate to share with them. Our role as mature, informed adults is to make decisions in their best interests. Our kids may not always agree with or like what we do, but that comes with the territory of being a parent.

While we value the thoughts, feelings, and opinions of our children, some conflicts, particularly those between adults, are inappropriate to share with them.

One critical way to shield kids from adult conflict is to establish boundaries. That is, the remarried couple must set boundaries for their relationships with each other, former spouses, relatives, and friends, especially with those who may have influence on the children. For instance, perhaps you and your spouse set a boundary to never argue in the presence of your kids. Arguing and fighting in front of them can have a profoundly negative, long-term impact.

If arguments happen frequently or they are hostile, physical, aggressive, or include stonewalling, silent treatment, or insults, it can definitely be harmful to children. Children who are exposed to this type of conflict will often become anxious, distressed, sad, angry, and depressed. These feelings result in sleep disturbances, poor performance at school, and difficulty focusing. In the longer term, these kids may become unable to manage conflict and form healthy adult relationships.[15]

While we cannot control what any adult might say or do in front of our kids when we're not around, we can agree that in our home, we will do our best to communicate with other adults, including our current and former spouses, with patience and maturity. We know this is nearly impossible at times, but as we have previously mentioned, we must remember that our former spouse is our child's parent too. We are not to impose our opinions about our ex onto our child. It's up to the children to make up their own minds about the attitudes and behaviors of their other parent, and in time, they will do just that.

Other adults in our lives, such as family and friends, probably invested in our first marriage in some capacity and have their own feelings and opinions about the dissolution, so we may very well have to relay our boundaries to them too. We can express our concerns and respectfully ask them to be kind and careful about what they say around the children. Maybe you don't want them discussing with your kids the divorce, your former spouse, or their stepparent or stepsiblings. Those are perfectly reasonable, appropriate boundaries. And as the old adage goes, "If you don't have anything nice to say, then don't say anything at all."

Another adage that is appropriate when it comes to shielding kids from adult conflict is "Don't damn them with faint praise." In other words, any insincere or hollow praise of a former spouse will often come across as criticism or sarcasm, which sends a negative message to kids.

We are called to love one another despite whatever has happened. For our own well-being and for the children's sake, we need to be gracious and allow the Holy Spirit to help us as we fumble our way through tough times. We can do this with God's help.

Take Action

Identify three boundaries that the two of you would like to establish to protect your children from adult conflict.

Jesus, you love children and want them to come to you, know you, and love you. Protect our children and please teach us to keep them safe as you would.

42

Forgiveness

If we confess our sins to him,
he is faithful and just to forgive us our sins
and to cleanse us from all wickedness.

1 John 1:9 nlt

In a previous chapter, we discussed the importance of loving one another. A critical component of putting that love into practice requires us to forgive not only ourselves but also others, especially those who have hurt or disappointed us. I, Ron, was blessed to witness the power of forgiveness through a man whom we'll call Harry.

I met Harry through the most influential mentor in my life, a physician named Dr. Johnson. Dr. Johnson had phenomenal medical wisdom, and he was also an amazing servant who cared deeply about his patients. Harry was one of Dr. Johnson's patients and had stage four terminal cancer. Harry confided in Dr. Johnson that he carried remorse about some of the things that had happened in his life. I don't know all the details, but I know that he was married, divorced, and married again and had a stepson whom he had neglected.

Harry asked Dr. Johnson to pray for him. Not only did the doctor do that, but he also invited me to accompany him on a visit to Harry's home. We visited him a number of times and invited others to join us. We all saw that Harry was wracked with grief and remorse. Nearing the end of his life, Harry needed forgiveness for what he had done and not done. We prayed for and with him, and he was ultimately able to find forgiveness and freedom before he died.

Harry was a model for all of us, teaching us the power of vulnerability. He bravely shared his regrets and his sins and asked for help. That small group of men who had been with Harry continued to meet on a weekly basis, which spawned other groups. Because of Harry's honest admission of his need for forgiveness fifty years ago, so many people have gone on to find freedom in Christ.

We all have things we regret, and for some of us, that regret is a heavy and painful burden to carry. We may regret things we said or did in our first marriage (or the current one), or perhaps we feel guilty about things we know we should have done or done better. Of course, not all of our pain and regret will be related to marriage, but it nevertheless affects us in the present.

As difficult and uncomfortable as it may be, we are called to forgive the people who have hurt us, including our former spouse. As Jesus teaches us, "Forgive us our debts, as we also have forgiven our debtors" (Matthew 6:12 NIV). We can't change people or the past, but Christ's forgiveness empowers us to forgive others. When everything else is gone, it is our relationships that remain. And any unreconciled relationships are like wounds in our hearts, minds, souls, and bodies.

We can't change people or the past, but Christ's forgiveness empowers us to forgive others.

The truth is that we all need Christ's forgiveness. We come humbly to him with our burden of sin, and he comes gracefully to us to forgive and cleanse us. As this chapter's Scripture verse promises, he is faithful to do his part, but we must do ours. Our part is to specifically identify what we need forgiveness for and confess it to him.

Take Action

Focus your prayer on forgiveness today. Ask God to forgive you. Ask God to help you forgive those who have neglected, hurt, and disappointed you. Remember there is nothing we can do to separate us from God and his love. Work to forgive others as Christ Jesus has forgiven you.

Thank you, Lord Jesus, for forgiving my sins. Help me to forgive others with the same grace and love that you have shown me.

43

Easing Anxieties

Don't worry about anything; instead, pray about everything. Tell God
what you need, and thank him for all he has done. Then you will
experience God's peace, which exceeds anything we can understand.
His peace will guard your hearts and minds as you live in Christ Jesus.

Philippians 4:6–7 nlt

Anxiety, as we all know, comes and goes. We sometimes experience
it in short flashes, and other times it crashes over us in huge waves,
overwhelming us entirely. Anxiety is normal; it's part of our humanity.
And it's certain that anxiety will creep into a remarriage and blended
family at some point (and likely many points), as both of these lifestyle
changes introduce all kinds of potential new concerns: Am I truly prepared and ready for a second marriage? Will my kids come to respect
and appreciate my new spouse? Will our kids ever get along? What is
my plan if this second marriage doesn't work out?

When we are anxious, our irritability and frustration affect
other people, especially family members. It can trigger emotional melt-
downs and spark interpersonal conflicts with the people we love and
care about most. We must learn how to cope with the unique stressful
situations presented within the contexts of remarriage and blending
a family.

First, get to the root of your anxiety. Ask yourself: What core
issue is making me anxious? For example, are you upset by something
your new spouse said or did that you felt was hurtful or inappropriate,
or are you more upset at the thought of having to confront them

about it? If you and your former spouse struggled to work through conflict, then it makes sense that you might feel anxious having to work through these same situations with a new partner. Nevertheless, getting to the bottom of your anxiety and naming it will give you a place to start to come up with solutions.

Focus on what's within your control and let go of what's not. Easier said than done, we know. You cannot control the feelings or behaviors of others, so it's not worth wasting your time and energy trying to do so. What you can control, however, is your own reaction. Maybe your former spouse is not as concerned with your kids' diet as you are. You can't make your ex buy healthier foods, but you can prepare nutritious meals for your kids when they're with you.

You cannot control the feelings or behaviors of others, so it's not worth wasting your time and energy trying to do so. What you can control, however, is your own reaction.

Identify patterns. For example, if you find yourself consistently getting stressed when your kids and your spouse's kids inevitably butt heads, work with your partner to establish a plan for how you will work through it. Maybe the plan is for an adult to call a time out, separate the kids, and talk to each child individually. Maybe you and your spouse prefer to sit the kids down together to work through it. Identifying patterns is a proactive way to anticipate tough situations and construct action plans to better equip you for the next incident.

Take action. Do whatever you can to bring relief to the situation at hand. Let's say that you offended one of your stepchildren and feel awful about it. You can't take it back, so there's no use in stewing over your mistake. Instead, address it, apologize, and ask the child for forgiveness. Not only will this resolve your anxiety, but it also illustrates to your stepchildren that you respect them and care about their feelings.

Further, it models accountability to them. It shows them that you're not afraid to confront your mistakes and learn from them.

Take care of yourself. In moments of chaos, conflict, and confrontation, slow down, settle down, rest, and breathe. Pausing and taking a step back to regulate your own emotions gives you an opportunity to gain perspective and consciously decide how you want to react. Part of this self-care could be talking to your spouse and praying together.

Ask for God's help. Jesus gives us an amazing invitation to turn to him when we are anxious: "Come to me, all you who are weary and burdened, and I will give you rest. Take my yoke upon you and learn from me, for I am gentle and humble in heart, and you will find rest for your souls. For my yoke is easy and my burden is light" (Matthew 11:28–30 NIV). Jesus is our companion, our Shepherd, and our leader as we navigate our way through anxiety.

Take Action

Revisit the surrender cycle from chapter 16.

Lord Jesus, the yoke you have for me is an easy and light one. When life feels like a heavy burden, remind me to come to you, for in you and only in you will I find rest and peace.

44

Maintaining Unity

Always be humble and gentle. Be patient with each other, making
allowance for each other's faults because of your love. Make every
effort to keep yourselves united in the Spirit, binding yourselves
together with peace.

<small>EPHESIANS 4:2–3 NLT</small>

Most remarried couples feel torn between their relationship and the
many needs for which they're responsible, such as kids, jobs, and
housework, to name a few. How can we keep our relationship strong
and stay unified as a couple when we have so many other pressing
responsibilities? The truth is that unity requires nurturing, which
means we must consciously commit and tend to our relationships. In
this chapter, you'll learn tips that worked for us and the couples we've
counseled over the years.

Schedule time together and spend it well. Choose a regularly
recurring date night, lunch, or morning coffee to add to your calendar.
It can be once a week, twice a month, or more if your schedule and
resources permit, and it doesn't need to be a lengthy amount of time.

We used to walk around a local lake on Wednesday evenings for
about an hour without the kids. It was a special time to catch up and
focus on us. We both looked forward to this time together, and it relayed
the message to our kids that our time as a couple was important to us.
It also allowed us to model to our children what it looks like to prioritize
couple unity, which benefitted them in their future relationships.

Don't let anyone or anything interfere with this time—just as you wouldn't for an event, such as a business meeting or a medical appointment. When we would tell others that we were unavailable because we were already scheduled for a date with our spouse, most people reacted with surprise. But people were understanding and occasionally expressed a little jealousy, wishing they had the same kind of commitment in their schedules.

Once you secure precious time together, be careful that you don't spend it talking only about your kids, work, or problems. When we would go on our walking dates around the lake, we were intentional about focusing on us, relaying our needs, and expressing how we felt about each other. The goal for alone time is to be sure you and your spouse feel close and connected to each other, so whatever you choose to do, make sure you put your phones away and practice active listening.

Again, remain a united front. You may be used to making decisions by yourself, but now you must make decisions together, whether they are about your home, work, finances, or even your children or your partner's children. If your spouse is cooking spaghetti for dinner and one of the kids complains, have your chef's back and say something like this, "I know spaghetti isn't your favorite, but it's what we're having for dinner tonight."

You may not always agree with your partner's ideas, plans, or decisions, but you must support one another. If you want to keep an open discussion and avoid defensiveness or a potential argument, you can say, "I don't think I agree with your decision, but I will do my best to support it and to support you."

You may not always agree with your partner's ideas, plans, or decisions, but you must support one another.

Romance your partner. Remember the excitement and butterflies you'd get for each other while dating? That's romance, and it's still around! It can be overshadowed by responsibility and stress, and over time it becomes easy to slide into a monotonous routine, but don't get too busy or comfortable with one another to forget the little things. Buy flowers, leave a sweet note in a lunch bag or on the mirror, or send a text during the day that simply says, "I miss you," or "I'm thinking about you." A kiss and embrace when leaving the house or coming home never get old either.

You can also build romance into your life by engaging in activities that you both enjoy. And if you like different things, then take turns planning the fun, and don't be afraid to try something new. It can be a powerful bonding experience to engage in an activity that your partner enjoys. And if you don't consider yourself much of a romantic, ask your partner what romance means to them, then try to meet their needs.

Take Action

Schedule your regularly recurring date and put it on your calendars. Below are five conversation starters to help you get going.

- What about me are you most thankful for this week?
- What three qualities most attracted you to me when we first met?
- What three qualities of mine most attract you now?
- What is the most challenging thing you're facing right now?
- What is energizing you right now?

Loving God, help us to always stay close to one another, make time for one another, and make each other a priority. Amen.

45

Marriage Assessment

Is there any encouragement from belonging to Christ? Any comfort from his love? Any fellowship together in the Spirit? Are your hearts tender and compassionate? Then make me truly happy by agreeing wholeheartedly with each other, loving one another, and working together with one mind and purpose.

PHILIPPIANS 2:1–2 NLT

From time to time, it is important for couples to jointly assess how they feel about their relationship. The purpose behind these kinds of assessments is not to complain or blame one another for what's not working. It's also not a time to deny or minimize areas in need of improvement.

From time to time, it is important for couples to jointly assess how they feel about their relationship.

In fact, it can be a time to celebrate all that is *good* in the relationship. It could even become a tradition on your wedding anniversary. Just an idea! But before you do the assessments below, remember the next three verses of Philippians 2: "Don't be selfish; don't try to impress others. Be humble, thinking of others as better than yourselves. Don't look out only for your own interests, but take an interest in others, too. You must have the same attitude that Christ Jesus had" (vv. 3–5).

In your journal or on your computer, copy the statements below. Next to each statement, write *yes* if it feels true or *no* if it does not. Then share your answers with your partner.

1. We listen to each other.
2. We enjoy being together.
3. We have fun together.
4. We express our affection for each other.
5. We affirm each other.
6. We trust each other.
7. We quickly forgive each other.
8. We laugh together.
9. We feel spiritually united.

A healthy marriage is one in which both partners' needs are met. Let the questions below serve as prompts to begin a positive, productive discussion about each other's needs.

1. How do you feel about our relationship today?
2. What is your greatest fear about our relationship?
3. What brings you joy or makes you smile when you think about me?
4. What motivates you to stay in our relationship?
5. What hope(s) do you have for our relationship?

Take Action

Read together Jeremiah 29:11: "'I know the plans I have for you,' declares the Lord, 'plans to prosper you and not to harm you, plans to give you hope and a future'" (NIV). And if you haven't already shared with one another your responses to the above questions, plan a time to do so.

Thank you, Lord, for our marriage. Please continue your graceful work in both of our lives and refine us so that we can be loving, supportive spouses to each other.

46

Seeking Professional Help

"I will ask the Father, and he will give you another advocate to help
you and be with you forever—the Spirit of truth...the Advocate, the
Holy Spirit, whom the Father will send in my name, will teach you all
things and will remind you of everything I have said to you."

JOHN 14:16–17, 26 NIV

We all journey through seasons of life: getting married, getting
divorced, remarrying, becoming a parent, having a great job, losing a
great job, enduring seasons of illness, and enjoying seasons of health.
From each season, we gain wisdom and perspective.

Marrying again is a season unlike any other. It elicits mixed feelings of joy, stress, hope, and anxiety and comes with ups and downs,
wins and losses. It brings moments during which we feel like we're in
heaven and moments when we feel like we are in a hell of a place,
feeling burnt out, confused, and ready to run away.

Just like we see a dentist or a doctor for our health, we can and
should seek help for the wellbeing of our marriage. Seek an objective professional in the form of a counselor or therapist to help you
and your spouse work through any serious, recurring, or unresolved
problems that you're experiencing. A counselor will provide insight,
perspective, and wisdom and guide you through tough conversations.
They can help you identify patterns, develop solutions, and teach you
and your spouse how to communicate effectively, equipping you to
solve future problems independently as a couple.

Seek an objective professional in the form of a counselor
or therapist to help you and your spouse work through
any serious, recurring, or unresolved problems that you're
experiencing.

Finding the right counselor takes time, discerning prayer, and research. Ask your friends, your pastor, or perhaps your attorney for personal recommendations. Most counseling practices have websites, but be sure to read the entire website. Pay attention to the counselor's background, experience, philosophy, and process to ensure that they resonate with you and your values. That is, if you want a counselor with a faith perspective, read carefully so as not to be deceived by vague spiritual language.

Look into the costs and find out how much coverage your insurance plan will provide to be sure it's affordable for you. Note that many marriage counselors are willing to schedule one listening session with you without charge. Check the counselor's location, too, to avoid having to travel a great distance. Nowadays, most every practice can schedule virtual appointments. Though perhaps not ideal, those sessions can be equally productive and make scheduling much more convenient.

For your first counseling session, be prepared to share a brief summary as to what brings you into their office. What do you need, what is your goal, and what do you hope to accomplish within that session and beyond? Be honest. If your marriage is in deep trouble, be frank about it. A good counselor will have the training, experience, and skill to address your immediate needs and develop a long-term strategy for tackling bigger issues. Be attentive in that first session to determine if you feel heard and understood by the counselor, as this indicates whether they're a good fit for you.

When I, Ron, went through my divorce, I was devasted and preoccupied with insecurity, loneliness, and fear, mostly around the wellbeing of my children but also about my future. After much prayer and help from friends, I was led to David, a counselor who was the perfect fit for me. David continually reassured me that I was going to make it through the hardship. He was kind, affirming, approachable, and compassionate.

In David, God gave me the gift of a wise servant who knew me, my heart, and my needs for survival. I now cry tears of gratitude that I made it through that dark season, and those tears remind me of God's love for me and how he was with me during every single one of those hard days.

As this chapter's Scripture passage promises, Jesus will send you the ultimate Counselor to teach you all things. When both you and your spouse are willing to listen, you will hear his voice, and he will guide you through challenging seasons one day at a time. One moment at a time.

Take Action

Share your honest feelings with each other about whether you need professional help. If you agree that you need help and feel ready to pursue it, talk and pray together about who that person could be. Commit to doing your research to find a good fit.

We thank you, our Father, Jesus our Savior, and the Holy Spirit our Counselor, for the gift of your presence, guidance, and wisdom. Help us turn to you for help in all the seasons of life. God, bless us and protect us.

47

Spiritual Nurturing

"I have come that they may have life,
and have it to the full."

JOHN 10:10 NIV

People who have been divorced often identify a lack of spiritual commitment as a reason for the breakdown of their marriage: "After we got married, my spouse stopped going to church with me...We never prayed together or talked about our spirituality." Whether this was a missing link or not, our souls need spiritual nurturing through our relationship with God, both as individuals and as couples.

Each of us was designed to have a relationship with our Creator, and God wants this relationship with us more than we want it with him. This spiritual relationship is like having wind in our sails. Without wind, we can't move, explore, create, or enjoy the journey. Wind in the sails brings life, renewal, power, and movement. And while many of us are raised with religion and may already have a relationship with a church, some of us do not yet know how to have a deep, personal relationship with God.

Jesus gently invites us to come to him: "I stand at the door and knock. If you hear my voice and open the door, I will come in" (Revelation 3:20 NLT). When we open the door and invite him into our lives, we begin our relationship with him. Like any supportive, loving relationship, we spend time together talking and listening on a day-to-day basis. We bring our joys and burdens to him as we would in any relationship, knowing that he understands our challenges and will give us the direction, guidance, and confidence that we need.

Our personal relationship with Jesus is important, and so is our relationship with him as a couple. Every couple needs spiritual nurturing, especially in remarriages, as most remarriages and stepfamilies present a surplus of unique, complex stressors that require more time, consideration, and energy.

Rather than talking about our circumstances, which tends to lead us nowhere or to disagreements, we often choose instead to pray together about whatever we're struggling with. Our next chapter offers details on how to do this, but ultimately, we remember that Jesus promises us this: "Come to me, all you who are weary and burdened, and I will give you rest" (Matthew 11:28 NIV).

Coming to Jesus together alleviates us from the burden of fixing and solving everything on our own and allows us to trust our circumstances to him. It unites us as a couple rather than dividing us. When we are humble enough to admit that we don't always know what to do or say and instead turn to God for direction, our marriage and our entire family benefit because God always directs us to do and say what is right.

Coming to Jesus together alleviates us from the burden of fixing and solving everything on our own and allows us to trust our circumstances to him.

Take Action

Think about the qualities and activities that make your relationships good ones. No doubt, you'd include quality time, talking, listening, honesty, vulnerability, and trust. These same things make for a real relationship with God. They don't happen once a week at church or whenever you happen to think about it. Open the door to a close relationship with God in which you schedule quiet time alone with him each and every day. Invite him in. Talk to him. Listen to him. Read his Word.

Lord, thank you for coming to the door of my heart and life and inviting me to be with you. Thank you for taking my burdens and giving me hope, trust, and peace.

48

Praying Together

There is one Lord, one faith, one baptism, one God and Father of all,
who is over all, in all, and living through all.

EPHESIANS 4:5–6 NLT

For partners who are already strong in their personal faith, sharing that faith together as a couple becomes key. This may be a new venture, as some of us feel that our faith is a private thing only between God and ourselves. But sharing the most private and personal parts of us demands trust and vulnerability, which are the building blocks of true intimacy. And true intimacy is what makes and keeps a marriage rock solid.

When Ron and I got married, he suggested that we commit to praying together on our knees every night. I had never prayed out loud with anyone, and it was a little scary. Still, I agreed. We knelt by our bed each night and took turns talking out loud to God, praying for each other and our family and sharing what was on our hearts. In those special times, we learned a great deal about what was going on with each other—what we were anxious about, struggling with, and joyful over.

We also prayed in thanksgiving for one another, for our children, for our health, and for all the gifts that God blessed us with. We wove our friends, family, and extended family into our daily prayers too. It was awkward at first but became natural over time. Now we sometimes pray together in the car or on a walk, or we'll stop whatever we're doing to pray a short prayer out loud. It's become a source of great joy and unity for us and is vital to our spiritual life together.

What we talk to God about usually represents the most private parts of us, so to invite another person to listen in on our conversations with him is to trust another person in the most intimate of ways. It is precisely this level of trust and vulnerability that builds true intimacy in a relationship.

What we talk to God about usually represents the most private parts of us, so to invite another person to listen in on our conversations with him is to trust another person in the most intimate of ways.

Praying together and asking God to guide us whenever life throws challenges our way has further helped us surrender to God but now as a couple. We have had and will continue to have conflicting ideas about decisions and plans. There will always be "my way" and "your way," but we also know what matters most: God's way. When we pray to him together, we each surrender "our way" and ask him what he wants for us and our family. And it unites us while we wait for his answer.

Take Action

If you have never prayed together as a couple, commit yourself to taking the risk to do it. Perhaps you can start by sitting or kneeling together, holding hands, and praying the Lord's Prayer or any other prayer you've both memorized. You could also take turns reading from a prayer book if that's less intimidating.

Eventually, you might feel comfortable praying in your own words. Simple ways of easing into a joint prayer like this can begin with "Lord, please help us…" or "Thank you, God, for…" Hearing each other's voices will help to get over the initial awkwardness.

Lord, teach us to pray together. Help us push through the awkwardness and fear. Help us trust that you will guide us in the decisions we have to make each day. Help us to let go of our own way and learn to trust your way—together.

49

Anticipating Good Fruit

"The seed that fell on good soil represents those who hear and accept God's word and produce a harvest of thirty, sixty, or even a hundred times as much as had been planted!"
MARK 4:20 NLT

God gave us a spouse to love and to plant seeds with. We plant seeds of faith in anticipation that good fruit will come from investing our time, emotion, affection, presence, and prayer—not only in our spouse but also our children and the generations to come. We plant these seeds in the hope that they, too, will go on to lead prayerful, faithful lives as spouses and parents.

We plant seeds of faith in anticipation that good fruit will come from investing our time, emotion, affection, presence, and prayer—not only in our spouse but also our children and the generations to come.

Investing in our spouse, children, and stepchildren is the best investment we can ever make. Every moment spent with them, individually and together, plants seeds of love, security, affirmation, and respect. These seeds will grow and produce a harvest. We might not necessarily see that harvest in our lifetime, but eventually the harvest will come. Remember that we walk by faith, not by sight, and faith comes from hearing the Word of God.

We personally have remained diligent about planting good seeds in our family by doing our best to model a good marriage, showing them that good marriages are possible. By our example of respect, acceptance, patience, and affection with and for one other, we have planted seeds of security in our children and shown them what a healthy, although not perfect, marriage looks like. We prioritized prayer, reading Scripture, and discussing passages together as a couple and with our children. We trust they will carry these seeds into their own marriages and their own parenting practices by living out the behaviors and attitudes that we modeled to them.

Something that we frequently tell remarried couples is that, yes, we all must deal with the day-to-day tasks and challenges that come up in life, but we also need to keep our eyes on the horizon, trusting that good things will come. Turn to the promise in Proverbs for reassurance: "Start children off on the way they should go, and even when they are old they will not turn from it" (22:6 NIV).

We don't stop planting until the day we are called home to heaven. In good times and in bad times, we keep planting. Our life is the life of a seed sower. Each day, one day at a time, we plant seeds, anticipating that good fruit will someday come from our faithful planting.

Take Action

Invest in your family by consciously planting a good seed today. Spend quality time as a family. Plan one-on-one time with each kid. Affirm each child on something specific today. Share with them the gifts and talents you see in them and encourage them to keep using those gifts. Pray for good fruit to come and actively anticipate it.

Help us, Lord Jesus, to grab every opportunity that comes our way to plant seeds of love, your love. Give us the faith to hope and trust that our entire family now and for generations to come will know, love, and serve you.

50

Lessons Learned

If you accept my words and store up my commands within you, turning your ear to wisdom and applying your heart to understanding—indeed, if you call out for insight and cry aloud for understanding, and if you look for it as for silver and search for it as for hidden treasure, then you will understand the fear of the Lord and find the knowledge of God. For the Lord gives wisdom; from his mouth come knowledge and understanding.

PROVERBS 2:1–6 NIV

Throughout this book, we've covered a wide range of experiences, emotions, and challenges common to remarriage and family blending. We've shared our expertise, our advice, our personal experiences, and the experiences of our clients. Now we'd like to neatly summarize for you five overarching lessons and key takeaways that you can carry with you into your new marriage and blended family.

Express gratitude to your spouse—every day. Marrying again and blending a family are anything but easy ventures. You'll both make mistakes and let each other down at times. That's okay; you're human. By voicing your appreciation for your spouse, you encourage one another and reinforce how much you value each other. This will go a long way in fortifying your connection during tough times. And remember that while you juggle the moving parts of a blended family, your relationship as a couple must always remain the top priority.

Get comfortable with vulnerability. Being vulnerable with each other demonstrates that you trust each other, and trust builds intimacy.

Stay in touch with your feelings and share them with your spouse. Share your fears, your frustrations, your wins, and your losses. Remain respectful in your sharing, especially if what you're saying could be interpreted as (or plainly is) criticism. Cushion every criticism with at least three praises. And if things get heated, try not to let the sun set on anger or any other negatively charged feeling between you. It can be tough to set aside your hurt and pride to prioritize your relationship, but that's vulnerability.

Listen, listen, listen. Remember when we discussed active listening and emotional accessibility? Those are both priceless communication skills because half of all communication is listening. Beyond auditory listening is listening to your body. Keep track of your energy levels and plan accordingly. If you've had a particularly exhausting week, don't pack your weekend full of social events unless those are energizing for you. Pay attention to your spouse's energy levels too. If the two of you have plans but you see that your spouse is tired or worn out, suggest staying home and relaxing together instead. Whether your spouse chooses to or not, you're showing them that you are paying attention and that you care about their wellbeing.

Practice patience. Patience with your spouse. Patience with your kids and your stepkids. Patience with the family blending process. Patience with change. Patience with yourself. Remarrying and blending a family are, in all likelihood, unchartered territories for you and your new spouse. Give everything and everyone the necessary time and space to grow. You are remarried for a lifetime, but live it out one day at a time, even one hour at a time some days.

Give everything and everyone the necessary time and space to grow.

Waste no time. Our time on this earth is so brief, and we never know when we're going to be called home to heaven. Share your love with your spouse and kids as often as you can. Hug them first thing in the morning. Tell them how much you adore them on their way out the door. Show up to their games and be their loudest cheerleader. Cook their favorite meals. Surprise them with thoughtful gifts. Plant those good seeds.

Take Action

Of the five lessons, choose at least one to put into practice today.

God of wisdom, remind us to turn to you for the day-to-day direction that we need. For in you alone do we find the understanding and insight to live fulfilling lives that please you.

51

Supporting Others

Praise be to the God and Father of our Lord Jesus Christ, the Father of compassion and the God of all comfort, who comforts us in all our troubles, so that we can comfort those in any trouble with the comfort we ourselves receive from God.

2 CORINTHIANS 1:3–4 NIV

We want to express our gratitude for all the good work that God is doing within us, and we can do that by sharing Christ's love with others. In other words, you can use your personal experience to be the person who provides care and compassion for someone else going through a divorce, remarrying, or blending a family.

Use your personal experience to be the person who provides care and compassion for someone else going through a divorce, remarrying, or blending a family.

One of the most powerful ways to support others who are going through major lifestyle changes is to be present for them. Make yourself available and be ready to listen. Let them speak freely and without judgment, remaining quiet and letting them lead the conversation. Others might feel less inclined to talk about it, in which case don't pressure them or ask a lot of questions. Sometimes our presence alone is enough to comfort someone.

Do practical things to help them through this stressful time of change and confusion. Bring them a meal or take them out to dinner. Offer to watch their kids so that they can take their new spouse on a date. Help them pack if they're moving. Take them shopping for new clothes if they're reentering the dating pool. All these efforts show them that they're not alone and that someone cares for them.

Encourage self-care. Are they exercising? Invite them into your fitness routine if you have one. Are they eating healthy or ordering takeout every night? Are they getting sufficient rest? Ask them how they're managing their stress. Take initiative in helping them. Don't wait for them to ask.

Be a long-term friend. Stay close. Pray for them and with them and check in on them frequently. Remind them of the fact that God has a plan for their lives. Share this Scripture for encouragement:

> "Do not be afraid, for I have ransomed you. I have called you by name; you are mine. When you go through deep waters, I will be with you. When you go through rivers of difficulty, you will not drown. When you walk through the fire of oppression, you will not be burned up; the flames will not consume you. For I am the Lord, your God, the Holy One of Israel, your Savior...Others were given in exchange for you. I traded their lives for yours because you are precious to me. You are honored, and I love you. Do not be afraid, for I am with you. I will gather you and your children from east and west. I will say to the north and south, 'Bring my sons and daughters back to Israel from the distant corners of the earth. Bring all who claim me as their God, for I have made them for my glory. It was I who created them.'" (Isaiah 43:1–7 NLT)

Take Action

Is there someone who has walked with you through tough, confusing times in your life? What did they say, do, or not say or do that was helpful to you? Is there someone for whom you could do the same in at least one simple way today?

Lord, sometimes I wonder why you seem to allow hard things in my life, but I know that you are with me and have something to teach me in these times. Help me to see it, learn it, appreciate it, and use it to love and support others going through similar challenges.

52

Worth the Challenge

All praise to God, the Father of our Lord Jesus Christ, who has blessed us with every spiritual blessing in the heavenly realms because we are united with Christ. Even before he made the world, God loved us and chose us in Christ to be holy and without fault in his eyes. God decided in advance to adopt us into his own family by bringing us to himself through Jesus Christ.

<small>EPHESIANS 1:3–5 NLT</small>

You may wonder if marrying again is worth the challenge, if there's a reward for being a stepparent, if it's worth the investment of time and energy, if it's a challenge at which you can succeed. Remember that, as a Christ-follower, you have been blessed with every spiritual blessing in the heavenly realms. One of those spiritual blessings is the gift of marriage, entrusted to you by our heavenly Father.

Because we are united with Christ, we are holy and without fault in his eyes. We are adopted into his own family. This is how and why we can enjoy the journey. He appointed us to be joined together to build an amazing family and reach out to other blended families, reminding them of Jesus' love and his blessing to delight in a loving marriage and family. And dare we say this: Christ has allowed us to marry again so that he can use us to share our stories, experiences, and what he has done and is doing in us despite our sins and failures of the past.

Jesus said, "I have told you this so that my joy may be in you and that your joy may be complete. My command is this: Love each other as I have loved you" (John 15:11–12 NIV). Our joy will be complete when we are loving each other as Jesus loves us. He expressed his love by laying down his life for us. He tells us to lay down our lives for our friends. That includes our spouse, kids, stepkids, and relatives. Our joy comes from giving of ourselves and dying to ourselves.

Our joy will be complete when we are loving each other as Jesus loves us.

You have been gifted with the privilege to partner with someone who understands, supports, and encourages you in your endeavor to be a great spouse, parent, and stepparent. The journey is unquestionably worth the challenge. Thank God and run the race. Persevere in giving and loving so that you ultimately hear the words "Well done, good and faithful servant!" (Matthew 25:23 NIV).

Take Action

Identify and celebrate some of the great things you have accomplished as a couple, as parents, and as stepparents. Share with each other what gives you the most joy about your relationship.

Lord God, thank you for blessing us richly and giving us the gift of each other. Thank you for guiding us, encouraging us, and adopting us into your family.

Acknowledgments

Thank you to Carlton Garborg, president of BroadStreet Publishing, for his wisdom, vision, leadership, and persistent encouragement.

Thank you to Nina Rose, our great editor, for her creative, encouraging, and insightful editing.

To the entire team at BroadStreet Publishing, we are grateful for your expertise and support in making this book a reality.

We also thank the leaders of the eye-opening workshop we attended before marrying and the support group that walked with us in the early years of our marriage.

Endnotes

1   Yerís H. Mayol-García, Benjamin Gurrentz, and Rose M. Kreider, "Number, Timing, and Duration of Marriages and Divorces: 2016," Current Population Reports, P70–167, U.S. Census Bureau, Washington, DC, 2021.

2   "Stepfamily Statistics," The Stepfamily Foundation Inc., accessed March 8, 2022, https://www.stepfamily.org/stepfamily-statistics.html.

3   Kim Parker, Juliana Menasce Horowitz, et al., "The American Family Today," Pew Research Center, December 17, 2015, https://www.pewresearch.org/social-trends/2015/12/17/1-the-american-family-today/.

4   You can access the National Christian Counselors Association at https://www.ncca.org/.

5   "Finishing Your Grieving: A Key to Life after Divorce," Up to Parents (website), accessed on October 18, 2022, https://www.uptoparents.org/view-article.aspx?articleid=12&language=1.

6   Terry Gaspard, "10 Rules for a Successful Second Marriage," The Gottman Institute, September 23, 2016, https://www.gottman.com/blog/10-rules-successful-second-marriage/.

7   Ann Gold Buscho, PhD, "How and When to Introduce Your New Partner to Your Kids," *Psychology Today* (website), May 10, 2022, https://www.psychologytoday.com/us/blog/better-divorce/202205/how-and-when-introduce-your-new-partner-your-kids.

8   Ginger Gentile, "Blended but Not Broken: Stepfamilies," *Forbes* (website), April 21, 2021, https://www.forbes.com/sites/gingergentile/2021/04/21/blended-but-not-broken-step-families/?sh=17ced1b941e7.

9   You can learn more about the Arno Profile System at http://www.apsreport.com/WhatisAPS.html.

10   Elisa Morgan and Carol Kuykendall, *Children Change a Marriage: What Every Couple Needs to Know* (Grand Rapids, MI: Zondervan, 2002), 32.

11   "Statistics: Children & Divorce," Owenby Law, P.A., October 11, 2018, https://www.owenbylaw.com/blog/2018/october/statistics-children-divorce.

12   "New Baby in a Stepfamily," Family Lives, last updated October 2022, https://www.familylives.org.uk/advice/your-family/stepfamilies/new-baby-in-a-stepfamily?referer=/advice/your-family/stepfamilies.

13   "Kids, Divorce, and School Success," Great Schools, October 29, 2020, https://www.greatschools.org/gk/articles/kids-divorce-and-school-success/.

14   Anna Sutherland, "How Parental Conflict Hurts Kids," Institute for Family Studies, April 9, 2014, https://ifstudies.org/blog/how-parental-conflict-hurts-kids.

15   Melissa Benaroya, "Is It Ever Okay to Argue in Front of the Kids?" Gottman Institute, September 30, 2021, https://www.gottman.com/blog/is-it-ever-okay-to-argue-in-front-of-the-kids/.